THE NICHE CODE

Rajeev Roy's entrepreneurial journey began in the trenches of real-world business, not in a corporate boardroom. After pursuing his MBA from IIM Ahmedabad, he ventured into entrepreneurship, successfully building and exiting ventures across diverse industries, including food processing, knowledge process outsourcing, dairy products and microfinance. These hands-on experiences shaped his deep understanding of the challenges in building and scaling businesses – insights that now define his work as an educator and mentor.

Recognizing the lack of structured support for early-stage entrepreneurs, Rajeev transitioned to entrepreneurship education in 2005. Since then, he has trained over 1,000 entrepreneurs and 300+ educators, mentored more than 100 start-ups and advised leading corporations on product development, leadership and innovation. His mentorship and incubation programmes have supported founders of some of India's most prominent start-ups, including Campus Sutra, Bewakoof, Practo, Thick Shake Factory, Hammer, VsnapU, Vahak and Ras.

His impact extends beyond India, spanning fourteen countries across five continents. He has established six incubators and accelerators in four nations. In Oman, he led the development of the world's first Arabic-language entrepreneurship programme, now implemented across all universities and colleges in the country.

In India, he has been instrumental in strengthening the start-up ecosystem. As the founding CEO of 36Inc in Raipur, he scaled it into the country's second-largest incubator, supporting over 100 start-ups in its first year alone. Later, as the founding dean at the XLRI Xavier School of Management, Delhi-NCR, he achieved an unprecedented milestone – leading the institute to a top ten ranking in its very first year. Under his leadership, XLRI Delhi-NCR launched an MBA in entrepreneurship, now attracting over 30,000 applicants per cohort, positioning it as the most sought-after entrepreneurship programme globally.

He is currently the Director of Firstbridge, a new-age business school focused on technology and emerging businesses.

THE NICHE CODE

Building Big Businesses In Small Markets

RAJEEV ROY

MACMILLAN BUSINESS

First published 2025 by Macmillan Business
an imprint of Pan Macmillan Publishing India Private Limited
707 Kailash Building
26 K. G. Marg, New Delhi 110001
www.panmacmillan.co.in

Pan Macmillan, The Smithson, 6 Briset Street, Farringdon, London EC1M 5NR
Associated companies throughout the world
www.panmacmillan.com

ISBN 978-93-6113-500-2

1 3 5 7 9 8 6 4 2

Typeset in Petursburg by R. Ajith Kumar, New Delhi
Printed and bound in India by Thomson Press India Ltd.

FSC www.fsc.org MIX Paper | Supporting responsible forestry FSC® C010615

To my parents, Rashmi and Ramesh Roy,
who taught me to be fearless and to believe in myself
– qualities that the entrepreneurs in this book embody
time and again.

CONTENTS

Introduction: The Age of the Niche ix

Why

1. The Small That Wins: How Niches Create Giants 3
2. The Big Trap: Why Scale Isn't Always the Answer 19

Who

3. The Hidden Map: The Many Shapes of a Niche 39
4. India: Land of a Million Niches 71
5. Hunting the Unseen: How to Spot the Perfect Niche 86
6. The Right Bet: Choosing a Niche That Works 108

How

7. More Than a Product: Crafting a Niche That Sticks 129

8. Built for the Few, Loved by Many: Niche Product Strategies 148
9. The Story You Sell: Branding, Pricing and Perception 173
10. Finding Your Path: The Channels That Make Niches Work 190

What Next

11. From Fringe to Front Page: How Niche Brands Go Mainstream 223
12. The Next Wave: Where Niches Are Headed Next 247

Acknowledgements 265
References 267

INTRODUCTION

THE AGE OF THE NICHE

For decades, entrepreneurs were taught a single mantra: scale or die.

From MBA classrooms to boardrooms, from *Shark Tank* pitches to venture capital term sheets, the logic seemed simple. Big markets meant big opportunities, and if your idea couldn't target millions, maybe even billions, it wasn't worth pursuing. The winners, we were told, were those who could dominate categories, crush competitors and flood every household with their product.

And yet, the story playing out around us is very different.

Many of today's thriving businesses often didn't start by going big. They started by going deep. Instead of chasing mass-market dreams, they began with a precise understanding of a particular customer, a specific frustration or an overlooked community. They didn't launch as household names. They became indispensable to a few – and grew from there.

These are businesses built on *niches*. And today, they're the ones rewriting the rules.

The Quiet Power of Small

Take a walk down an aisle – online or offline – and you'll see it. Forest Essentials sells luxury Ayurvedic beauty products rooted in tradition. Paper Boat bottles Indian nostalgia in a sleek modern pouch. boAt took on global audio giants with products built for the new-age Indian. Zerodha reimagined stock trading by making it cheaper and simpler for retail investors. Yoga Bar turned health food from an afterthought into an alternative lifestyle.

These companies didn't win by trying to please everyone. They won because they spotted an unfulfilled need and owned it. Deeply.

In the early 2000s, if you wanted to build a personal care brand, you were up against Unilever and P&G. If you wanted to launch a tech start-up, you needed servers, serious funding and expensive advertising. Today, you can build a direct-to-consumer (D2C) brand from your bedroom, use AI tools to find your first hundred customers and tell your story on Instagram without spending a rupee on television advertising.

The gatekeepers have lost their monopoly. The tools are in your hands.

But while it's easier than ever to start a business, it's harder than ever to be spotted in the crowd. Attention is scarce. Algorithms are unpredictable. Trends arrive and fade within weeks. In this environment, scale without clarity is a trap. It's focus, not frenzy, that wins.

From Obsession to Opportunity

Niche businesses aren't small because their founders lack ambition. They're focused because their founders have conviction. These are people who care deeply about a problem, an idea or a community, and they're willing to build for it when no one else is paying attention.

This is not about chasing trends. It's about spotting patterns others miss. Understanding needs others overlook. Serving people whom others dismiss.

In writing this book, I've spoken to founders who built brands out of jackfruit, ancient Odia rituals, crochet hooks, a love for chess and even school uniforms. I've seen small-town entrepreneurs create global audiences. I've seen obscure family traditions turn into full-fledged businesses.

These aren't flukes. These are signals. A shift is underway, and it's changing how business is built.

A New Playbook

The Niche Code isn't a theory. It's a practical, modern playbook for how small markets create big businesses.

This book is built from the ground up – shaped by conversations with founders, years of mentoring entrepreneurs and the hands-on experience of building and investing in businesses across India and beyond. It draws on case studies that are fresh, not overused. It avoids the usual Silicon Valley clichés and brings in real, relevant stories from our context.

Each chapter tackles a fundamental part of the niche-building journey:

- Why scale can be a trap, and how staying small at first can be your strength.
- How to recognize the shape of your niche, whether you're selling high-end fashion or industrial spare parts.
- Why India is uniquely suited for niche businesses, thanks to its complexity, diversity and fragmentation.
- Where to look for great niche ideas, including underserved communities, emerging habits and hybrid markets.
- How to choose the right niche, based not just on market potential, but on your fit as a founder.
- What it takes to build a product that matters, not just one that sells.
- How branding, storytelling and pricing turn small businesses into cult followings.
- Which are the platforms, communities and tools that will help you find and grow your tribe without relying on huge budgets.

- How niches grow: organically, logically and, sometimes, counterintuitively.
- What the future holds, as AI, digital access and global demand reshape the playing field.

This is not a book of hacks and tricks to get rich quickly. It's about principles that endure. It's about building something real and doing it in a way that's aligned with who you are and who you want to serve.

Who This Book Is For

If you're an entrepreneur looking to start something new, this book will help you avoid the pitfalls of the scale-at-any-cost mindset.

If you're already running a small business, this book will sharpen your positioning, deepen your connection with customers and grow without losing your soul.

If you're a student, a homemaker, a freelancer or a side-hustler, this is your permission slip to start small, start specific and start smart.

If you work in a large organization, this book will help you spot new growth opportunities that your competitors can't see. It will help you innovate from the edges, not the centre.

And if you're simply someone who loves business – its stories, its people, its power to solve real problems

– I hope this book is a fresh lens on what success can look like.

Why This Book Matters Now

We live in a time of overload: too many choices, too much noise, too much sameness.

In that world, what we crave is not more generic options, but meaning.

Niche businesses offer that meaning. They reflect our values. They solve problems in ways that feel thoughtful and personal, not generic and off-the-rack. They feel like they were built for us ... because they were.

Technology is an enabler, not a replacement. AI can detect your target customers. E-commerce will help you reach them. But it's still your clarity, mission and empathy that will make them stay.

This is the golden age of niches. Whether you're selling handcrafted notebooks or business-to-business (B2B) automation tools, whether you're in Bhubaneswar or Berlin, your ability to define your niche – sharply, honestly and boldly – will define your success.

A few final things.

Every successful business begins with a *choice.*

Not a product. Not a campaign. Not a pitch deck.

A choice to serve someone clearly, deeply and with care.

This book is an invitation to make that choice.

To reject the myth that bigger is always better.

To believe that small can be powerful.

To realize that focus is not a limitation – it's your superpower.

Welcome to *The Niche Code*.

Let's get started.

WHY

1

THE SMALL THAT WINS

HOW NICHES CREATE GIANTS

A first-time visitor to a Zostel is often surprised by the experience. It doesn't feel like a typical hotel check-in. There's an air of informality, a subtle shift from the transactional to the personal. The staff doesn't just greet you; they welcome you as if you've arrived at a friend's house. The rooms are compact and utilitarian – many with shared bunk beds – but there's a deliberate charm to the way everything is arranged. Fellow travellers, scattered about the space, seem to exude a sense of ease. Smiles are exchanged freely, making you feel like a part of the larger community.

The real magic, however, lies in the common areas. This is where Zostel's spirit comes alive. Some travellers are huddled over a Google map, planning their day's adventures. Others are deep in conversation, swapping travel stories. A few are lounging with books or catching up on social media updates. All around you, there's a hum of connection. Every corner is a visual delight: a boho swing strung between two trees, a little bubbling spring nestled in a zen garden. It's Instagrammable, yes, but it's also deeply intentional. Every detail is crafted to encourage interaction, spark curiosity and plant the seeds of a shared experience.

This is Zostel, a pioneer of backpacking culture in India. Founded in 2013, it wasn't just a business idea; it was a movement. Inspired by the backpacker hostels of Europe, the seven co-founders sought to transplant that ethos into the Indian landscape. Their vision was clear: create not just a place to stay but a place to belong. The traditional hospitality industry, with its polished rooms and perfunctory service, catered to comfort. Zostel wanted to cater to people.

From the beginning, Zostel's founders made unconventional decisions. They didn't turn to traditional hotel managers or hospitality experts to shape operations. Instead, they sought those who *understood* travellers – particularly the young, free-spirited backpacker who prioritizes experiences over opulence. They created shared spaces designed to foster interaction and connection: communal kitchens, open lounges and dormitories that encouraged conversation rather than isolation. Their goal wasn't to compete with luxury hotels or budget lodges but to carve out a new space defined by human connection and shared adventure.

But Zostel's real genius lay not just in understanding their market but in narrowing it down further. While the broad category of 'backpackers' was a good starting point, the founders knew they needed to go deeper. Within that community, they identified a specific group that was both underserved and deeply in need of what they were offering: solo female travellers. These were women who sought freedom, adventure and exploration, but often hesitated to travel freely due to safety concerns and the lack of traveller-friendly infrastructure tailored to their needs.

Zostel decided to build its entire experience around this specific customer profile. They created spaces that made solo female travellers feel secure: female-only dorms, well-lit common areas, 24/7 security, secure lockers and staff trained to handle emergencies. Even their marketing and communication strategies were crafted to resonate with this audience. The messaging spoke directly to solo female adventurers, assuring them that Zostel wasn't just a hostel. It was a sanctuary.

The strategy worked. By 2024, Zostel had expanded to more than 110 locations across India and achieved revenues exceeding ₹200 crore. More importantly, nearly 60 per cent of their guests were solo female backpackers. That translates to over 5,00,000 solo women travellers so far – a staggering testament to their ability to understand and serve a niche market.

This is the power of the niche. Zostel didn't try to appeal to everyone. Instead, they zoomed in on a distinct category of travellers who were hungry for a customized solution. In doing so, they created not just a product, but an experience – and, ultimately, a community.

A niche market is not just a smaller piece of the larger marketplace; it's a carefully carved-out space where specificity reigns supreme. Think of it as a focused subset of a sprawling, noisy crowd – a pocket of individuals bound together by unique needs, tastes or preferences that mainstream businesses often overlook. In the grand tapestry of consumer demands, niches are threads that add texture, detail and depth, bringing vibrancy to what might otherwise feel generic.

Take, for instance, a fashion brand that makes trousers for tall people or a café that caters exclusively to pet owners. At first glance, these ideas may seem insignificant, even frivolous. But they echo a profound truth: specificity builds intimacy. By narrowing their focus, these businesses can create a sense of belonging that mass-market competitors simply cannot replicate.

In a world where customers are inundated with choices, the most meaningful connections often come from the details. Niche markets thrive on differentiation – the understanding that what appeals to one group might not resonate with another. Their greatest strength lies in harnessing the power of specificity: the ability to forge loyalty and enthusiasm among a small, tightly knit audience.

This is the secret behind Zostel's success and the lesson for aspiring entrepreneurs: when you find the heartbeat of a specific group, you don't just build a business – you build a home for your customers.

What Exactly Is a Niche?

We often think of a niche as a subset of a larger marketplace. But in reality, a niche is far more than that – it's a deliberate act of focus. It's characterized by the decision to pay attention to what others overlook. A niche is like a hidden path in a dense forest, leading to a group whose problems remain unsolved. It's not just about finding customers, it's about understanding them.

For instance, the founders of Zostel could have simply aimed for 'budget travellers'. That's a big category: broad, vague and easy to market to. But they didn't stop there. They zoomed in. They identified solo female backpackers, a group who craved adventure yet often hesitated because the world didn't seem to have been designed with them in mind. By narrowing its focus, Zostel wasn't shrinking its market; it was creating a movement.

A niche, then, is not a demographic or a random segment of the population. Targeting 'millennials' isn't a niche. Targeting 'millennial pet owners who want organic dog food delivered to their door' is. The first is a label; the second is an insight.

At the same time, a niche isn't simply a quirky idea. It's not about being different for the sake of it. A café that sells coffee infused with turmeric may get attention, but unless that turmeric coffee solves a problem or satisfies a specific longing, it's just a gimmick. A true niche is purposeful because it connects with people on a level that feels both personal and essential.

The Origins

The idea of a 'niche' feels so familiar in the business world that it's easy to assume it was born there. But its roots stretch far beyond to the natural world, where survival is a game of precision, not brute force. In ecology, a niche isn't just a market segment – it's a species' entire way of life. It dictates what it eats, where it sleeps, how it competes and how it thrives.

Biologists describe this in terms of niche width, i.e. the range of conditions a species can tolerate and the resources it can use. Generalists, like raccoons, thrive across a broad spectrum, eating anything from discarded pizza to freshwater mussels. Specialists, on the other hand, operate within much tighter constraints. The koala has evolved to feed almost exclusively on eucalyptus leaves. It may seem limiting, but in reality, this specialization gives it an advantage – no competition, no distractions, no wasted energy chasing after anything else. It has carved out a space in which it is unrivalled.

This brings us to a fundamental law of ecology: the Competitive Exclusion Principle, which dictates that two species competing for the same resources cannot coexist indefinitely. One will inevitably outcompete the other. In business, the same rule applies. When two companies offer indistinguishable products to an identical set of customers, a battle for dominance begins – one that often ends with a clear winner and a vanquished rival. It's the reason you rarely see two thriving grocery stores at the same street corner, why once-mighty brands like Nokia and BlackBerry crumbled under the weight of direct competition and why start-ups that position themselves head-on against giants often find themselves swallowed whole.

But nature offers another path: resource partitioning. Different species avoid direct competition by carving out their unique roles. Some birds forage in the treetops; others hunt closer to the ground. Plants with deep roots extract water from deeper soil layers, leaving the upper layers to those with shallow roots. This is how species coexist. And this is also how businesses survive. Instead of battling for the same customers with the same offering, start-ups can thrive by claiming a sliver of the market that larger players overlook.

Consider how Tesla first entered the auto industry. Instead of taking on Ford or Toyota by launching a mass-market car, it started at the high end with an electric sports car for wealthy early adopters. Stripe didn't launch as an all-encompassing financial services firm; it specialized in making online payments easy for software developers. Zoho didn't try to be another Microsoft. It targeted small- and mid-sized businesses that wanted cost-effective, cloud-based enterprise software.

This is the power of specialization. A start-up that defines its niche with precision isn't just avoiding competition – it's making itself indispensable. And if the industry's biggest players ever decide to encroach on its turf, the specialist, much like the koala, will be far better equipped to defend its territory.

Category Creators

In 2002, Ravi Modi stood on a bustling street of Kolkata, surrounded by a sea of small shops and tailors promising to stitch the perfect sherwani. This was how things had always been done: the fabric was chosen at one store, the design painstakingly explained to a tailor and then came the endless fittings, adjustments and time-consuming visits. It wasn't just a process – it was a ritual, one that catered to those who had the time, money and patience for it. Ravi Modi looked at this and thought: *This isn't just inefficient – it's exclusionary.*

Liberalization had opened up India's economy, and with it, a wave of middle-class professionals whose lives now revolved around packed office schedules and demanding workweeks. They were ambitious, aspirational and decidedly short on time. For this group, spending weeks getting a sherwani stitched for a wedding wasn't just inconvenient, it was nearly impossible. And yet, there was no alternative.

That's where Modi saw his opening.

Manyavar wasn't just another clothing store; it represented a new way of thinking. For the first time, Indian men could walk into a store and pick up a ready-made sherwani – stylish, affordable and instantly available. It was the antithesis of the traditional tailoring process, and that struck a chord. By 2025, Manyavar had grown into a ₹20,000-crore brand with over 600 stores. Modi had not just launched a brand; he had created a new category of fashion – ethnic festive wear – where none had existed before.

The same story played out in another corner of the world with a company called Airbnb. Before Airbnb, the concept of staying in someone else's home while travelling was relegated to a dusty corner of Craigslist – a functional but uninspiring option for homeowners looking to make a quick buck while they were out of town. It wasn't a market so much as a fleeting idea.

But Airbnb changed everything.

From its humble beginnings – listing a single San Francisco apartment – Airbnb redefined the way people thought about travel. Offering an alternative to hotels, it turned homes into destinations, hosts into ambassadors and travellers into part-time locals. By 2025, with 8.1 million active listings worldwide, Airbnb wasn't just a company; it was the category leader and had become a name that had become synonymous with the niche itself.

What ties Manyavar and Airbnb together isn't just their success – it's the way they changed the rules of the game. When you uncover a niche, you're not merely finding an underserved audience; you're opening the door to an entirely new way of doing business. It's a chance to evolve into what business thinkers call a 'category creator'.

A category creator doesn't settle for competing within an existing framework; they invent their own. While others look for incremental improvements – better pricing, faster delivery, bigger scale – category creators focus on differentiation. They see the overlooked and underserved and ask: *what would happen if we built something entirely for them?*

The magic of discovering a niche lies in its transformative potential. At first, a niche feels like a quiet, overlooked corner of the market. But once you begin to carve your path, the space stops feeling small. It starts to expand, drawing more and more people in. The rules aren't dictated by your competitors anymore. They're yours to write.

Category creators don't fight for a slice of the pie; they bake an entirely new one. By redefining what the market values, they become indispensable. That's the true power of a niche. It doesn't simply allow you to exist in the marketplace – it lets you shape it. And before long, what started as an idea for the few becomes a movement for the many.

In the wilderness of untapped opportunities, discovering a niche isn't just about finding a new path. It's about creating one that others never even saw.

What a Niche Strategy Entails

The most successful niche strategies don't just happen. They are built with intention, step by step, on three key pillars:

Empathy and Understanding

A niche strategy begins with asking the right questions. Who are your customers? What keeps them up at night? What makes them smile? And, perhaps most importantly, what's missing from their lives? This kind of understanding requires more than surveys or data – it demands empathy. It's about listening to people, not as numbers or segments, but as human beings with specific, unmet needs.

In its early days, Airbnb wasn't trying to compete with every hotel chain or vacation rental company. Instead, it focused on a particular type of traveller who wanted authentic, affordable and localized experiences.

By understanding this group's frustrations with generic hotel stays and their desire to feel 'at home' wherever they travelled, Airbnb carved out a niche that ultimately disrupted the global hospitality industry.

Crafting Tailored Solutions

A niche isn't just about identifying a specific group; it's about creating something *for them.* This means designing products, services and experiences that reflect an in-depth understanding of your audience's world.

Manyavar revolutionized how Indian men shop for wedding and festive outfits. They didn't try to compete with traditional clothing stores or high-end designers. Instead, they focused on middle- and upper-middle-class grooms who wanted stylish, ready-to-wear ethnic outfits without the hassle of custom tailoring. By addressing their specific needs – affordability, style and convenience – Manyavar built a brand that became synonymous with Indian weddings.

Focused Messaging and Connection

A niche strategy requires speaking directly to your audience in a language they understand. It's about building a relationship, not just making a sale. The words you use, the platforms you choose and the tone you strike should all demonstrate a deep connection with your customers' lives.

Zostel didn't position itself as a generic hotel chain. Its messaging was targeted and deliberate. It spoke to the aspirations of young travellers looking for connection and specifically solo female backpackers searching for safety and freedom. Every Instagram post, every piece of content felt like a personal invitation to join a like-minded community.

Why Start-ups Need a Niche Strategy

Every company, whether a sprawling multinational or a neighbourhood shop, needs a strategy to carve out its place in a niche market. But for start-ups, this isn't just important – it's a ticket to survival. The giants can afford to dabble and test the waters with resources to spare. Start-ups don't have that luxury. They need focus. They need an edge. And more than anything, they need a niche where they can play to their strengths before the bigger players even notice they exist.

Focus Beats Scale

Start-ups, by their very nature, lack the resources to compete with giants. Trying to serve everyone is a quick path to failure. A niche strategy allows them to focus their energy where it matters most. Instead of being mediocre at many things, they can excel at one thing.

La Sportiva is an Italian sports shoe company, but it does not try to serve all sportspeople. It makes shoes for mountaineers, hikers and skiers. By focusing specifically on them, it has created a brand identity that resonates with their target market.

Intimacy Breeds Loyalty

Customers in niche markets often feel ignored. When a start-up recognizes and validates their needs, it creates an emotional connection. This isn't just a transaction – it's a relationship. Loyal customers are more likely to return, recommend your offering and advocate for your brand.

Airbnb didn't just provide cheaper stays; it created a sense of community. Hosts and guests felt part of a shared experience, and that sense of belonging turned users into ambassadors.

The Freedom to Innovate

A niche strategy permits start-ups to experiment. When your focus is narrow, you can try unconventional approaches, test bold ideas and refine your product based on direct feedback from your audience.

A Foundation for Growth

A common misconception is that niches are limiting. But in truth, they're launching pads. By mastering one niche, start-ups create a strong foundation to expand into related areas.

Airbnb started with budget-conscious travellers looking for short-term stays in shared spaces. Over time, it expanded into luxury rentals, long-term stays and experiences. Yet it never lost sight of its core promise: authenticity and connection.

Depth Over Breadth

The difference between a niche strategy and a mass-market approach is simple: one goes deep, while the other goes wide. Mass-market strategies chase breadth – they try to appeal to as many people as possible, often by being as neutral as possible. But niches thrive on depth. They find a specific group and say: *we understand you better than anyone else.*

Zostel didn't succeed because it had the most beds or the biggest marketing budget. It succeeded because it knew its audience and built everything – the rooms, premises, safety features – with them in mind.

That's the lesson for start-ups. The path to success doesn't lie in trying to be everything to everyone. It lies in being everything to someone.

WHAT IS A NICHE?

A niche is not just a market subset; it is a focused, intentional space built around specific unmet needs and deep customer understanding.

Origin: From ecological 'niches' which protect species from direct competition

Category Creators: Brands like Manyavar and Airbnb created entirely new categories by recognizing and serving unmet needs in new ways.

Three Pillars of Niche Strategy:

1. **Empathy and Understanding**: Truly know your audience's unspoken needs.
2. **Crafting Tailored Solutions**: Design offerings that feel made for that specific group.
3. **Focused Messaging and Connection**: Communicate in a language that resonates personally.

Why Start-ups Need Niches:

- Focus beats scale. Do one thing brilliantly.
- Intimacy cultivates loyalty.
- Niches enable bold innovation.
- Small beginnings can lead to wide expansion.

The difference between a niche strategy and a mass-market approach is **depth over width**.

2

THE BIG TRAP

WHY SCALE ISN'T ALWAYS THE ANSWER

There's an instinct, ingrained in us from childhood: bigger is always better. The bigger slice of cake, the bigger pay cheque, the bigger house. In business, this instinct translates into market share, scale and reach. Bigger means more customers, more sales, more dominance. It's an idea that has fuelled corporate empires and shaped the strategies of countless start-ups. But what if this obsession with size is misleading? What if the pursuit of 'bigger' blinds us to smaller opportunities, but far more meaningful?

History is filled with cautionary tales of businesses that grew too fast, too broadly, and lost their way. Bigger is alluring because it's visible – it announces itself with large numbers and sweeping claims. But going bigger also comes with compromises, distractions and a dangerous dilution of focus. To understand why bigger isn't always better, we need to look at how size changes the dynamics of success and how start-ups, in particular, thrive when they embrace smaller, more deliberate ambitions.

The Illusion of Scale

The illusion of scale begins with numbers. A start-up reaches 1 million users, then 5 million, then 50 million. These milestones are celebrated as signs of success, but they rarely tell the full story. Are these users engaged? Are they loyal? Or are they simply part of a fleeting crowd, drawn in by marketing tactics and quickly lost to the next big thing? Scale can make a business look invincible, but it doesn't guarantee substance.

Take Paytm, for instance. It started with a clear, focused mission: simplify mobile recharges and bill payments. The value proposition was simple, and the market responded enthusiastically. But success bred ambition, and soon it ventured into everything – e-commerce, wealth management, gaming, ticket booking, even insurance. The app, once synonymous with convenience, became cluttered with additional features. Competitors like Google Pay and PhonePe, which focus on digital payments, began to outperform Paytm in terms of user retention and satisfaction. Scale became Paytm's blind spot, a shiny object that distracted them from the clarity of purpose it once had. This lack of focus, coupled with the Reserve Bank of India's (RBI) regulatory actions, has resulted in a drastic drop in share price. From an issue price of ₹2,150 in November 2021, it dropped to ₹395 in February 2024, and by July 2025, it had recovered only to ₹1,052.

Many start-ups scale prematurely, before they've truly validated their product or business model. This often leads to rapid expenditure without corresponding revenue growth, ultimately resulting in failure. The competitive landscape and customer expectations often shift as a start-up scales. What worked in a niche market may not be effective in a larger, more diverse market. Start-ups need to approach scaling realistically. They should focus on validating their core value proposition and building scalable systems and processes before aggressively pursuing growth.

The Complexity of Growth

Growth, by its nature, adds layers. More customers mean more data to manage, more services to deliver, more people to keep happy. Growth is often painted as an organic trajectory, but every step upwards also means stepping into greater complexity. And complexity, as it turns out, has a way of stifling what made you special in the first place.

Imagine a small, agile start-up. Decisions are made quickly, ideas are tested on the fly and adjustments are carried out without hesitation. Now imagine that same start-up five years later. It has a sprawling team, a global presence and an expanded product line. Decisions take weeks, even months. Innovation slows under the weight of processes and approvals. The company's early agility – once its superpower – has been traded for bureaucracy.

The EdTech giant Byju's is a case in point. It began as a disruptive force in education, making high-quality, app-based learning accessible to millions. But as its ambitions grew, so did its appetite for acquisitions. Byju's bought WhiteHat Jr., Aakash Institute and several other companies in rapid succession, aiming to dominate the sector. With each acquisition, the company's focus blurred. Complaints about aggressive sales tactics and a decline in user experience started piling up. What once felt like a mission-driven company began to resemble a corporate behemoth struggling to manage its own sprawling operations. The cost of growth wasn't just financial – it was existential.

Growth is not a linear process. It involves layered nuances related to people, processes, technology and strategy. Start-ups must be prepared to adapt and evolve as they grow. They need to transition from informal, ad-hoc structures to more formalized ones. This can be challenging, as it requires balancing flexibility with control. Hiring and retaining the right people becomes increasingly crucial. So does building a strong company culture and developing leadership capabilities. Scaling requires the standardization of processes and systems to ensure consistency and efficiency, a tricky curve for start-ups that are used to operating in a more improvisational manner. Rapid growth can sometimes stifle innovation. Start-ups need to find ways to preserve their innovative spirit while scaling.

The Cost of Growing Big

For start-ups, growth is often framed as a necessity. Investors demand it. Markets reward it. But what rarely gets discussed is the cost, both direct and indirect, of growing big – not just in terms of money, but in terms of energy, attention, and purpose. Start-ups need to be aware of these costs and manage them effectively to ensure sustainable growth.

Growth stretches resources thin. Teams become overburdened. The focus shifts from creating value to managing scale. In the rush to expand, corners are inevitably cut, and the customer experience suffers. The very traits that once set a start-up apart – its authenticity and connection with users – begin to erode.

Consider Meesho, a start-up that began with a compelling mission to empower small resellers in India. It struck a chord with homemakers and small entrepreneurs, offering a platform to grow their businesses through social media. But as Meesho grew, it tried to compete directly with giants like Flipkart and Amazon. The pivot claimed a price. In early 2022, Meesho's monthly cash burn was estimated to be around $40 million. In a bid to attract D2C buyers, they offered steep discounts and free deliveries. Soon, the once-focused platform was scrambling in a hyper-competitive market, losing its unique identity and struggling to achieve profitability. Growth, instead of being a strength, became a liability.

Rapid growth requires significant investment in areas like hiring, infrastructure and marketing. Start-ups must have a clear understanding of their unit economics and ensure that growth is profitable. As start-ups grow, their operational costs tend to increase. This can be due to factors like increased complexity, bureaucracy and the need for more sophisticated systems. Focusing on growth can sometimes lead to neglect in other important aspects, such as profitability or customer satisfaction. Start-ups need to carefully analyse the costs associated with growth and make sure that their growth strategy is sustainable in the long run.

The Cost of Trying to Be Everything

If the illusion of scale and the complexity of growth are traps, then trying to be everything to everyone is the most dangerous pitfall of all. It's a strategy rooted in fear – the fear of missing out on opportunities, on customers, on markets. But in chasing everything, a company often ends up with nothing.

Future Group is a cautionary tale. Led by Kishore Biyani, the group revolutionized Indian retail with Big

Bazaar, a chain that catered to middle-class families with affordable groceries and essentials. But success led to overextension. Future Group ventured into fashion, electronics, food processing and financial services, creating an extensive empire that became difficult to sustain. When the pandemic hit, the cracks became impossible to ignore. Debt piled up, operations faltered and the once-iconic brand had to sell off its assets to Reliance Retail. The lesson? Being everything to everyone is not just unsustainable – it's self-destructive.

WeWork's story offers an international parallel. The company started with a simple, elegant idea: shared office spaces designed for collaboration and community. It was a concept that resonated deeply with freelancers and start-ups. But CEO Adam Neumann's vision of turning WeWork into a lifestyle brand led to reckless expansion. The company ventured into education, wellness and even residential housing, burning through billions in the process.

When WeWork filed for its IPO in 2019, its financial mismanagement and lack of a sustainable business model came to light. The company's valuation plummeted from $47 billion to less than $10 billion, and Neumann was ousted. When WeWork filed for bankruptcy in 2023, its valuation fell to $44.5 million. The business became a cautionary tale of what happens when growth is prioritized over focus and discipline.

Expanding into too many markets or product lines

can lead to a loss of focus and difficulty in maintaining a clear brand identity. Offering a wide range of products or services can increase operational complexity and make it harder to manage the business effectively. Spreading resources too thin can lead to decreased profitability, as the start-up may not be able to achieve economies of scale in any one area. Start-ups should identify their core strengths and focus on doing a few things well, rather than trying to be everything to everyone.

Why Bigger Isn't Better for Start-ups

For start-ups, the temptation to think big is almost irresistible. Bigger markets, bigger teams, bigger impact – it's the dream sold by venture capitalists and celebrated in headlines. But the reality is often far more complicated. Bigger isn't always better. For many start-ups, bigger simply means more unwieldy, more expensive and more prone to failure.

Think about Instagram. When it was launched in 2010, it wasn't trying to be a platform for everyone. It was a niche product for photography enthusiasts, offering a simple way to share beautifully filtered photos. The team stayed small and focused, refining the product and listening closely to its users. This laser focus on doing one thing exceptionally well helped Instagram stand amongst competition that included Hipstamatic, Camera+, Picplz and others. By the time Facebook acquired it in 2012, Instagram had only thirteen employees but 30 million users. The lesson? Depth, not breadth, creates value.

Start-ups should prioritize validated learning and build a strong foundation to ensure that their growth is sustainable, profitable and scalable. Focusing on metrics like user numbers or website traffic without a clear path to profitability can create a false sense of progress. Trying to grow too quickly can distract start-ups from their core value proposition and make it difficult to maintain a competitive advantage.

Small Markets, Big Impact

The idea of starting small is often dismissed as unambitious, but some of the world's most successful companies began by focusing on niche markets. These markets, though seemingly small, provide a unique opportunity: they let start-ups build deep connections with their users and iterate quickly without the distractions of scale.

Take Zoho, for instance. The company started by creating a single product – an online word processor – long before Google Docs became a household name. Over the years, Zoho expanded its product suite cautiously, each time ensuring it delivered real value to its niche of small and medium businesses. Today, Zoho is a global player, but it didn't get there by trying to do everything at once. It got there by mastering the art of small markets.

Another example is Patagonia. The outdoor clothing brand didn't start by trying to dominate the entire apparel industry. It doubled down on high-quality gear for climbers and outdoor enthusiasts. By staying true to its core audience and values, Patagonia built a fiercely loyal customer base. It didn't need to appeal to everyone; its niche was more than enough to sustain its growth.

Start-ups, if they are to survive, must find the cracks – those overlooked spaces where industry giants have failed to tread. Nowhere is this more evident than in insurance, a world dominated by deep-pocketed incumbents and dense bureaucracy. And yet, a new breed of start-ups has emerged, not by taking on the behemoths directly, but by carving out niches so specific that they become, almost by default, the best in their domain.

Take Pie Insurance, based out of Salt Lake City in the USA. In 2021, at a time when venture funding had begun to dry up, Pie managed to raise an astonishing $315 million. Why? Because it focused on only one thing – workers' compensation insurance for small businesses. Not the wide-ranging, catch-all policies of legacy insurers, but precision-crafted coverage for a very particular customer.

Inclined, the brainchild of serial entrepreneur Mark Shaw, saw an opportunity in an even dustier corner of the industry: loans against whole life insurance policies. Traditionally, this was a process bogged down by paperwork and inefficiency. Inclined digitized it, streamlined it, and, in doing so, made itself indispensable.

Then there's Covertree, which insures prefab and modular homes, properties traditional insurers have long treated as outliers. Boundless Rider, meanwhile, caters exclusively to motorcyclists and power-sport enthusiasts, with an eye on becoming the go-to insurer for e-bikes.

None of these companies is trying to be everything to everyone. Instead, they've identified where the old system is weakest, set up camp and made themselves essential. In an industry built on broad one-size-fits-all policies, their power is their specificity.

Small markets don't just offer a foothold; they're a foundational proving ground where start-ups can refine their products, build their reputation and create a loyal customer base before taking on larger challenges. Airbnb, for instance, began by targeting conference attendees in San Francisco who couldn't find hotel rooms. That narrow focus allowed its founders to test their concept, gather feedback and gradually expand their vision. Today, Airbnb is a global giant, but its success was built on the back of small, focused beginnings.

Niche markets often have less competition than larger markets, making it easier for start-ups to gain traction. Focusing on a specific customer segment allows a deeper understanding of their needs and builds stronger relationships. These hyper-specific spaces can be highly profitable, as start-ups can often charge premium prices for specialized products or services. A loyal customer base in a niche market can help spread the word about a start-up through word-of-mouth marketing.

The Power of Restraint

Restraint might seem counterintuitive in a world that celebrates scale, but it's one of the most powerful tools a start-up can wield. Restraint means saying no when saying yes feels tempting. It means focusing on what matters most, even when opportunities to expand abound.

Restraint, in the context of start-ups, is the ability to resist the temptation to overspend, over-hire or overexpand. By exercising restraint, start-ups can conserve resources, maintain focus and increase their chances of survival.

Zoho exemplifies the power of restraint. Unlike many of its peers, Zoho has avoided external funding and has grown organically. The company doesn't chase trends or venture into markets where it can't add real value. This disciplined approach has not only made Zoho profitable but also deeply respected by its customers. Restraint, in Zoho's case, isn't about limiting ambition – it's about channelling it and staying true to its vision.

Apple's early years offer another compelling example. When Steve Jobs returned to the company in 1997, Apple was floundering, burdened by a bloated product line that confused customers and drained resources. Jobs's first move was to slash the product line-up by 70 per cent, focusing the company's energy on a handful of products that would define its future. The iMac, the iPod and, eventually, the iPhone, were born out of this ruthless focus. Restraint didn't hold Apple back; it propelled it forward.

Restraint in spending can help start-ups extend their runway and weather economic downturns. A focus on efficiency and lean operations can help maximize their resources, stay focused on their core mission and avoid distractions. A culture of restraint can foster a sense of discipline and resourcefulness within a start-up. It should be practised in all aspects of the business, from spending and hiring to product development.

Restraint also means knowing when to stop. It's the opposite of the 'move fast and break things' mentality that Silicon Valley often glorifies. Restraint says: move thoughtfully. Build carefully. Grow sustainably. For start-ups, this mindset can be the difference between becoming a flash in the pan and building something that lasts.

The Lesson: Focus Over Frenzy

In Olympic shooting, fractions of a millimetre decide champions. And if you've watched a rifle event in recent years, you've seen a logo that reads '10.9' stamped on the sleeves of the world's best marksmen. That's the logo of Capapie Sports, a company from Pune, and the man behind it is Nilesh Rane.

Rane wasn't born into the business of sports apparel. A shooter himself, he trained under India's legendary coach Sanjay Chakravarty. His entry into the sport was almost accidental – he wanted a shooting license because his grandfather owned a century-old hunting rifle. But once he started competing, he saw an edge hiding in plain sight: the shooting jacket.

Unlike other sporting gear, a rifle jacket isn't just another piece of equipment – it's the foundation of performance. Shooters lean back unnaturally, balancing on their heels, and the jacket stabilizes their body, reducing strain on muscles and bones. A fraction of an inch of extra rigidity can mean the difference between gold and oblivion.

In 1997, with no background in textiles, Rane sketched his ideal jacket and had a leather artisan stitch it together. He wasn't thinking about business; he was only concerned with his passion for the sport. But word spread. Shooters started calling. By 2014, after years of tinkering, he developed Capitex, a synthetic-canvas blend that offered unprecedented stiffness while complying with the regulations of the International Shooting Sport Federation.

The results? At the Tokyo Olympics, 70 per cent of rifle shooters wore Capapie jackets, winning eight of fifteen medals. By Paris, that number had climbed to 90 per cent, and fourteen of fifteen rifle medals were claimed by shooters wearing his design. With higher accuracy, scores have surged in the last two Olympic cycles, and many believe Capapie is the reason why.

What started as a personal experiment became the secret weapon of the world's best. In the hyper-precise world of rifle shooting, Rane didn't just improve the gear – he may have rewritten the sport itself. Even today, Capapie remains focused, and it dominates the niche it focuses on.

These cautionary tales underline a simple truth: bigger isn't always better. Companies that chase scale for its own sake often lose sight of their purpose and, in the process, alienate their core audience.

The lesson for start-ups is clear: stay grounded. Define your niche, focus on your strengths and grow deliberately. Growth isn't just about reaching more people – it's about reaching the *right* people in a way that creates lasting value. In the race to grow, don't lose sight of what made you unique in the first place.

The ideas discussed in this chapter challenge the conventional wisdom that growth is always the ultimate goal. For start-ups, success doesn't come from being the biggest. It comes from being the best at what you do. In a world obsessed with scale, sometimes the smartest move is to think small.

- **Bigger ≠ Better**: Growth is seductive but can lead to diluted focus, increased complexity and strategic missteps.
- **The Illusion of Scale**: Chasing scale too early – like Paytm's scattergun expansion – often sacrifices clarity of purpose and undermines core strengths.
- **Complexity Kills Agility**: As seen for Byju's, rapid growth creates layers of management, slows decisions and erodes innovation.
- **Cost of Scale**: Scaling demands energy, capital and compromises. Meesho's pivot to mass retail came at the cost of identity, community and profitability.
- **The Danger of Doing Everything**: WeWork and Future Group collapsed under the weight of overexpansion, trying to serve too many segments at once.
- **Small Markets, Big Wins**: Start-ups like Patagonia and Airbnb succeeded by starting small, staying focused and building deep user loyalty before expanding.

- **The Power of Restraint**: Companies like Capapie Sports and Zoho demonstrate how deliberate focus and disciplined growth can yield dominance in niche markets.
- **The Final Lesson**: Sustainable success doesn't come from being the biggest – it comes from being the most focused, authentic and valuable to the right audience.

WHO

3

THE HIDDEN MAP

THE MANY SHAPES OF A NICHE

A niche is not just a small market. It's a particular kind of small market, with its own rules, quirks and, most importantly, its requirements and implications for how a business should operate.

Take two niche businesses: Aerialworx does high-performance drone filming for filmmakers in UK, TailBlaze handmakes organic pet food for high-income dog owners in Mumbai. Both are niche, but they are nothing alike. The drone camera business is business-to-business (B2B), highly technical and requires deep industry knowledge. Its customers are few but extremely valuable, and once they're convinced, they tend to buy again and again. It's a niche that thrives on relationships, expertise and credibility. In contrast, the organic pet food business is a business-to-consumer (B2C) enterprise. It plays on emotional appeal and depends on broad but precise marketing. The challenge isn't deep expertise – it's building trust quickly, creating a strong brand and making repeat purchases a habit. Both are niche businesses. But one grows through deep specialization, while the other scales through strong branding and community-building.

So, what makes a niche a niche?

It turns out, not all niches are created equal. They vary in their size, reachability, complexity and price dynamics, and understanding these differences holds the key to mastering them. Some niches are small, but highly lucrative. Others are large but fragmented. Some demand technical expertise, while others succeed on pure brand power. Certain niches operate invisibly to the public eye, tucked away in B2B supply chains, while others are loud and visible, playing on social media trends and emotional connections. To understand how to choose, build and dominate a niche, you first have to understand its shape, i.e. the unique components that define what it is.

Because a niche isn't just where you play – it's how you play.

B2B Versus B2C

Imagine you run a business that makes high-performance drone cameras, not the kind that hobbyists fly in their backyard, but precision-engineered machines designed for filmmakers, real estate developers and defence contractors. Your customers aren't scrolling Instagram looking for impulse buys. They're industry professionals who carefully weigh their options and look for reliability, precision and long-term support.

Now think of the second business. This one sells organic, handcrafted dog food for high-income pet owners in Mumbai. Your customers aren't corporations. They're people who adore their dogs, see them as family and don't mind spending extra for fresh, human-grade ingredients. Your marketing isn't built on technical specs – it's built on emotion, storytelling and trust.

Both businesses operate in niche markets. But they play by completely different rules.

One exists in the slow-moving, expertise-driven world of B2B, where a single sale can take months to close but be worth lakhs, or even crores. The other thrives in the fast-moving, sentiment-driven world of B2C, where customers buy based on emotion, convenience and branding. Some businesses fit cleanly into any one of these categories. But many sit somewhere in between, straddling both worlds in ways that shape everything – from how they sell, how they price and how they grow.

The Silent Power of B2B Niches

B2B niches are invisible to the average person, but they are everywhere. If you ask a friend to name a famous coffee brand, they might say Starbucks or Nescafé.

But for a restaurant owner, the answer might be Kaapi Solutions, an Indian company that specializes in high-end commercial espresso machines. No one outside the industry talks about them, but for café owners, they're a must-know name.

That's the nature of B2B niches – they don't chase mass visibility. Instead, they focus on a small, highly specific customer base and become indispensable to them.

B2B niche businesses share some common traits:

- They have a few but valuable customers. Unlike B2C businesses that rely on thousands (or millions) of small purchases, B2B niches can thrive with a handful of high-value clients.
- Sales cycles are slow, but relationships last. It can take months to close a deal, but once a B2B customer commits, they tend to stay for years.
- Expertise matters more than brand. No one chooses an industrial robotics supplier based on clever Instagram ads. In B2B, what wins is technical know-how, trust and deep industry experience.

Take Lohia Aerospace Systems, a company that manufactures carbon fibre composites for military aircraft. You'll never see an ad for them on TV. But for defence contractors and government agencies, they are a critical supplier that operates in a highly specialized, deeply profitable niche. B2B businesses don't need viral marketing or mass-market appeal. They need credibility, patience and the ability to build long-term trust.

The Fast, Emotional World of B2C Niches

If B2B niches operate behind the scenes, B2C niches thrive in the spotlight. For B2C businesses, success isn't about technical specs or multi-year contracts. Rather, they focus on creating desire, building community and standing out in a crowded marketplace. Araku Coffee is an Indian brand that sells organic, single-origin coffee grown by tribal farmers. It's not competing with Nescafé or Bru on price or convenience. Instead, it's selling a story – of ethical sourcing, artisanal craftsmanship and premium quality. Customers aren't just buying coffee; they're buying a lifestyle, a belief system and a connection to something meaningful.

B2C niche businesses play by different rules:

- It's high volume and lower price per sale. Unlike B2B, where one deal can be worth lakhs, B2C niches rely on thousands of smaller purchases.
- Emotional branding is everything. People don't just buy organic skincare or handcrafted jewellery. They buy into their aesthetic, identity and aspiration.
- Marketing moves fast. B2C niches are trend-driven. They depend on social media buzz, influencer partnerships and storytelling to stay relevant.
- B2C niches are high-energy, fast-moving and constantly evolving. They can scale quickly, but

they also require continuous engagement to maintain momentum.

The Grey Area: Businesses That Blur the Line

Not every business can be neatly categorized into B2B or B2C. Some sit somewhere in between, serving both types of customers in different ways. Wakefit, the Indian mattress brand, started as a D2C company, selling affordable memory foam mattresses online. But as it grew, it saw another opportunity: supplying hotels, co-living spaces and corporate housing providers. Now, it operates in both B2C and B2B, with two different sales strategies running in parallel.

Consider Paper Boat, the niche beverage brand that brought traditional Indian drinks into modern packaging. It started as a B2C brand, targeting nostalgia-driven urban consumers. But soon, it found another market – corporate clients, airlines and hotels. Today, Paper Boat isn't just a consumer brand; it's also a bulk supplier to businesses.

These businesses didn't have to choose between B2B and B2C. Instead, they built two different growth engines, each reinforcing the other.

Which One Is Right for Your Niche?

Choosing between B2B and B2C isn't just about the product; it's about how you want to sell, expand and build meaningful relationships with customers.

- If you enjoy long-term partnerships, technical expertise and high-value sales, a B2B niche might be the way to go.
- If you thrive on brand-building, storytelling and fast-moving trends, then a B2C niche could be your ideal playground.
- And if your niche has potential in both worlds, you might be one of those rare businesses that can balance both markets and grow strategically on two fronts.

In the world of niche businesses, it's not about whether you play the game – it's about choosing the game that plays to your strengths.

How Big Is Small? Understanding the Size of a Niche

In 2008, a shop opened on San Francisco's Pier 39 that, at first glance, looked like a novelty store. Inside, you'd find scissors with reversed blades, notebooks with bindings on the right-hand side and ergonomic kitchen tools curved in the opposite direction of what you're used to. The name of the store? Lefty's: The Left Hand Store.

It was a store built for 10 per cent of the world's population: left-handed people.

At the outset, that might not sound like a niche at all. However, one in ten people is a huge number. That's nearly 800 million people worldwide. But the challenge isn't just numbers – it's distribution. There aren't enough left-handed people concentrated in one place to make a physical store a thriving, scalable business. That's why Lefty's is an iconic curiosity, a stop for tourists on a pier, not a global chain.

But other left-handed businesses have taken a different approach. Instead of relying on foot traffic in physical locations, they use the internet to aggregate demand globally. They sell left-handed school supplies in Australia, left-handed kitchen gadgets in Canada and left-handed guitars in Japan. They don't need all left-handed people to be in one place. They just need them to be online.

And that's the lesson of large niche markets:

- The numbers are there, but they are spread across the world.
- Scaling is not about local dominance – it's about finding your audience globally.
- The internet makes it possible to reach niche customers who, decades ago, would have been too dispersed to serve.

Large niches are counterintuitive. They have huge potential customer bases, but because those customers are scattered, success depends on distribution, discoverability and the ability to unify demand across geographies.

The Micro-Niche: When You Only Need a Few Customers

But some niches are not large at all. In fact, some are so small that they only have a handful of customers. And yet, those businesses thrive. Like NuScale Power, an American company that designs and manufactures small modular nuclear reactors. The market for this product is minuscule. Governments and energy companies don't buy nuclear reactors on impulse. They don't browse through reactor models on Amazon. The world has fewer than 500 active nuclear reactors, and decisions on new builds involve years – sometimes decades – of planning, regulatory approvals and political manoeuvring.

Yet, NuScale Power isn't exactly struggling.

Founded in 2007, it has reached a market cap of over $4.5 billion by 2025.

In B2B micro-niches, the value per customer is astronomical. If you only have ten potential buyers in the world, but each contract is worth billions, you don't need thousands of customers. You don't even need hundreds. You just need one deal to close every few years to be a wildly successful business.

This is the key lesson of small niche markets:

- You don't need a large customer base but a handful of high-value buyers.
- The focus is on expertise, credibility and long-term relationships.

- Success isn't about volume – it's about depth.

The nuclear reactor business couldn't be more different from selling left-handed notebooks. And yet, both are niche businesses. The difference is in how size shapes strategy.

What the Size of a Niche Means for Business Strategy

Whether your niche is big but dispersed or tiny but deep, the market size fundamentally changes how you approach the business.

If your niche is large but globally scattered:

- You need a way to unify demand. Selling online, building global logistics or creating an international franchise network is often the way forward.
- Distribution is more important than location. Lefty's in San Francisco is a cultural landmark, but the real money is in companies selling left-handed tools online to a global audience.
- Branding matters more than exclusivity. Unlike micro-niches, where businesses thrive in secrecy, large niche businesses need visibility and marketing muscle.

If your niche is small and highly specialized:

- Deep relationships matter more than broad outreach. If you only have ten potential buyers in the world, you don't need Facebook ads – you need personal meetings, industry credibility and regulatory approvals.

- Technical expertise is everything. Companies in micro-niches don't compete on branding; they compete on their knowledge, trust and problem-solving ability.
- The price per unit is high. Unlike left-handed notebooks, which sell for a few hundred rupees, a single NuScale Power contract is worth billions.

So, How Big Should Your Niche Be?

Choosing the right niche size isn't just about what sounds exciting – it's about understanding what kind of business you want to build.

If serving a passionate but globally dispersed customer base excites you, a large niche – like left-handed products, vegan protein or artisanal Indian tea – could be ideal.

If you prefer deep expertise, a slow but steady sales cycle and a business built on long-term contracts, a micro-niche – like aerospace components, scientific instruments or industrial robotics – could be the better bet.

Some businesses start small and grow bigger. Others stay small and dominate a lucrative niche forever. The key isn't just choosing a niche – it's choosing the right size niche for how you want to grow.

The Geography of a Niche: Everywhere or Just One Place?

If you've ever heard a blues guitarist break into a solo, or if you listen to Bollywood songs from the fifties, chances are you've heard the sound of a Hohner harmonica. It's the unmistakable wail behind some of the most legendary blues, Bollywood and rock performances in history, including those by musicians like Bob Dylan, Bruce Springsteen and Mohammed Rafi.

What's fascinating about Hohner isn't just that it makes harmonicas. It is that it makes *the* harmonica – the industry standard, the first name in the niche, the brand that dominates a global market of enthusiasts, hobbyists and professional musicians.

A harmonica is a small, inexpensive instrument, but the market for it isn't small at all. From street musicians in Paris to blues players in Chicago to folk bands in India, harmonicas are played all over the world.

Yet, the business of selling harmonicas isn't like selling Coca-Cola. It's not something every single person buys. It's a niche product with a globally dispersed but highly loyal audience.

And that's the defining characteristic of geographically unconstrained niches:

- The market is everywhere – but not concentrated anywhere. A single city can't sustain a business selling only harmonicas. The entire world can.

- The brand needs global reach to succeed. Selling a niche product in a fragmented market requires international distribution, strong brand recognition and the ability to unify demand across geographies.
- Marketing is about community, not location. Hohner doesn't advertise to 'the general public'. It sells to musicians, music teachers and harmonica enthusiasts – wherever they are.

That's how a company based in Trossingen, Germany, became the world leader in harmonicas, serving an audience that spans continents, cultures and musical genres. But not all niche businesses work like this. Some aren't global at all. Some are so geographically concentrated that they can only exist in one place.

The Power of a Hyper-Local Niche

Now, consider a business that cannot scale beyond a single city, town or even a neighbourhood – not because the market isn't big enough, but because the nature of the product itself is tied to a place.

Ernest Winzer Cleaners is a dry-cleaning business in New York City. There's no shortage of dry cleaners in New York, but Winzer isn't just any other dry cleaner. Since 1908, it has specialized in cleaning and maintaining the elaborate costumes used in Broadway shows and has continued to dominate this niche for over a century. Every major Broadway production, from *The Phantom of the Opera* to *Hamilton*, trusts Winzer to handle their delicate, custom-made costumes that can't be cleaned like a regular suit or dress.

This is the nature of hyper-local niche businesses:

- They succeed by being irreplaceable in one location. Winzer thrives because Broadway thrives. Its expertise is so specialized, and so trusted that no competitor has been able to challenge it.
- They rely on word-of-mouth and deep roots in the industry. Winzer doesn't need social media ads or massive marketing campaigns. It survives on reputation, legacy and relationships they've built within the Broadway community.
- They can command loyalty and pricing power. When a business is deeply tied to a specific place and industry, it often has a monopoly on expertise. People will pay a premium for that level of trust.

Hyper-local niche businesses can be extremely profitable, but they operate very differently from globally dispersed niches. They grow by going deeper, not wider – by owning a location instead of expanding to multiple ones.

What Geography Means for Your Niche Strategy

The geographical spread of a niche market fundamentally shapes how a business operates.

If your niche is globally dispersed:

- You need reach, not locality. Success depends on your ability to sell across borders, through e-commerce, franchises or strong distribution networks.
- Shipping and logistics matter. The ability to get your product to customers anywhere – fast and reliably – is as important as the product itself.
- Community is your market, not geography. The customers may be scattered, but if they share a common passion, identity or profession, you can build a strong brand.

If your niche is geographically concentrated:

- Your location is your brand. Customers come to you because you offer something unique to that place – whether it's food, services or a cultural experience.
- Word-of-mouth and deep local engagement are key. Your business needs to be woven into the fabric of the community rather than relying on digital marketing or mass distribution.
- Scaling means depth, not expansion. Growth isn't about opening across hundreds of locations – it's about becoming a local institution.

Where Should Your Niche Live?

Some businesses start globally dispersed and remain that way. Others begin hyper-local and expand cautiously. Some evolve from one model to another. Hohner, for example, could never have succeeded by selling harmonicas only in Germany. It had to think globally from day one. But Ernest Winzer Cleaners thrives by being the go-to service for an industry concentrated in a single location. Its strength is in its exclusivity. Choosing a niche isn't just about what you sell – it's about where your customers are. Because in niche markets, geography isn't just a backdrop – it's a strategy.

The Complexity of a Niche: Engineering or Simplicity?

In the world of niche businesses, not all products are created equal. Some require cutting-edge research, patented technology and deep industry expertise. Others thrive on insight, branding and execution. The difference between the two isn't just about what's being sold – it's about how the business itself is built.

To understand this, picture two very different companies.

One of them manufactures ejection seats for fighter jets. The other makes fashionable clothing for plus-sized women. Both serve niche markets. Both do well in their respective spaces. But the way they operate – and the challenges they face – couldn't be more different.

The Science of Survival: High-Complexity Niches

If you're a pilot in a military aircraft and something goes wrong, sometimes you have less than two seconds to get out before impact. That's where Martin-Baker, a British company that has spent decades perfecting the ejection seat technology, comes in. Founded in the aftermath of World War II, Martin-Baker's expertise is a matter of life and death. Their ejection seats have saved over 7,600 pilots, and they supply more than 90,000 seats to ninety-three air forces worldwide. This isn't a business built on branding or social media engagement. There are no viral TikToks about ejection seats. There's no influencer unboxing experience. Success in this niche comes from one thing: technical perfection.

This is what defines highly complex niche businesses:

- Customers don't buy on impulse. No one 'browses' for ejection seats. The sales cycle is long, involves intense scrutiny and often takes years.
- The barrier to entry is extremely high. You can't just start making ejection seats in your garage. Success requires decades of research, technicalities related to intellectual property (IP) and regulatory approvals.
- Trust is everything. If a Martin-Baker seat fails, lives are lost. The company doesn't compete on price – it competes on engineering, reliability and an unshakable reputation.
- In technical niches, you're not just selling a product – you're selling advanced know-how, credibility and the assurance that no one else in the world can do what you do.

But complexity isn't the only way to win in a niche market. Some niches aren't about engineering at all. Instead, they understand people.

The Power of Simplicity: Low-Complexity Niches

At first glance, the business of selling clothing for plus-sized women seems to have nothing in common with making ejection seats. But B Curve, an extension of the Indian fashion brand Berrylush, conducts its business just as effectively as Martin-Baker does.

Why? Because while Martin-Baker solves a life-or-death problem, Berrylush Curve solves a problem of identity, inclusion and self-expression.

For decades, mainstream fashion brands ignored plus-sized consumers. The designs available were dull, outdated or simply resized versions of standard clothes – without considering the actual needs and proportions of plus-sized customers. Berrylush saw the gap and filled it by launching an extension of their brand for plus-sized customers – not with complex technology, but with deep consumer understanding.

This is what defines low-complexity niche businesses:

- It's not just about innovation – it's about execution. The idea of plus-size clothing isn't new, but getting the fit, designs and brand positioning spot on is what sets Berrylush Curve apart.
- Speed matters more than exclusivity. Unlike Martin-Baker, where a product might remain the same for

decades, fashion trends shift constantly. The key to success isn't deep research – it's fast adaptation and staying ahead of consumer demand.
- The brand is more important than the product. Unlike ejection seats, which are chosen based on technical specifications, customers choose fashion brands based on how they make them feel.

Berrylush Curve's business isn't built on patents or engineering breakthroughs. It's built on a profound empathy towards the customer.

What Complexity Means for Business Strategy

Whether a niche product is highly technical or relatively simple changes everything about how the business is built.

If your niche is technically complex:
- You must invest in research and development (R&D) or own proprietary IP. If your product relies on innovation, you need to be the one driving it – or at least have exclusive access to technology that others can't copy.
- Your customers will be slow to adopt. But once they do, they will stay loyal to your products. Military aircraft manufacturers don't switch ejection seat suppliers every year. But it takes years of testing and credibility-building to win their trust.
- Your pricing power is strong. When a product is

technically complex, the price is determined by performance and reliability – not by competition in the open market.

If your niche is low in technical complexity:

- Execution matters more than invention. You don't need a patent to start a clothing brand, but you do need to differentiate on fit, design, brand identity and customer experience.
- Speed matters more than exclusivity. Unlike ejection seats, plus-size clothing trends change every season. Being able to move quickly, respond to customer demand and scale efficiently are critical.
- Your brand is your biggest asset. In low-complexity niches, customers don't make decisions based on technical specifications. They make decisions based on how a brand makes them feel.

Which Type of Niche Is Right for You?

Some businesses are built on technical breakthroughs. Others are built on cultural and consumer insights.

- If you're passionate about R&D, proprietary technology and solving complex problems, a technical niche might be your best bet.
- If you're more interested in brand-building, consumer psychology and fast execution, a non-technical niche can be just as lucrative and comes without the same barriers to entry.

Both approaches work. The key is knowing which game you're playing – before you start playing it.

The Challenge of Identifiability: Finding (or Being Found by) the Right Customer

If you're a woman in India who is pregnant, nursing or trying to conceive, chances are you'll hear about Nutrizoe. Maybe your doctor recommends it. Maybe another mother swears by it. Or maybe you stumbled across it while scrolling through Instagram, where a targeted ad for Lactobites, a snack designed to boost lactation, caught your eye.

Nutrizoe, India's pioneering women's nourishment brand, doesn't have to search far and wide for its customers. They are easily identifiable, clearly defined and actively looking for solutions. If you're pregnant, you know it. If you're struggling with lactation, you're aware of the struggle. There is no ambiguity in the customer's need. Nutrizoe doesn't have to create demand – it simply has to meet it.

The Power of a Clearly Identifiable Niche

A business like Nutrizoe operates in a niche where customers self-identify their requirements. The challenge isn't to find them – it's to convince them. And when the need is urgent, as in the case of pregnancy or lactation, conversion happens quickly.

This is what defines an easily identifiable and reachable niche:

- Customers know they have a problem. There's no need for heavy education or persuasion. A pregnant woman knows she needs better nutrition. A nursing mother knows she needs to boost her milk supply.
- The market can be highly segmented. Nutrizoe doesn't sell to 'women' in general – it sells to pregnant women, nursing mothers and women trying to conceive. Each subgroup has distinct needs, allowing for targeted product development and messaging.
- There are clear distribution channels. Nutrizoe reaches its audience through OB-GYNs, maternity hospitals, online mom communities and baby product retailers. There's no guesswork about where customers are or how to find them.

The business implications are profound. With a highly identifiable niche, marketing becomes laser-focused. Acquisition costs are lower, customer retention is higher and repeat purchases are built into the model. Lactobites, for example, sees a repeat rate of over 40 per cent – a dream metric for any consumer start-ups.

But what if your niche doesn't work like this?

What if your ideal customer doesn't know they need your product?

What if they're scattered across different demographics, hard to reach and even harder to convert?

The Challenge of an Unreachable Niche

Now, consider a completely different kind of business.

You run a company that specializes in providing personal security for high-profile individuals. Your clients are billionaires, celebrities and political figures – people who never respond to ads, rarely reveal personal information and operate with layers of privacy and exclusivity.

How do you reach them?

You can't exactly run a Google ad targeting 'VIPs who need better security'. You can't put up a billboard outside Mukesh Ambani's house. Your ideal customer is hidden behind layers of wealth, gatekeepers and discretion.

This is the sphere of World Protection Group (WPG), a firm that provides elite security services to high-net-worth individuals, A-list celebrities and corporate executives. Unlike Nutrizoe, where the target audience is actively searching for solutions, WPG's ideal customer never wants to admit they need security at all – until they do.

This is what defines a difficult-to-reach niche:

- Customers don't know, or won't admit, that they need your product. A billionaire won't publicly announce, *'I need a security overhaul!'* Privacy is their top priority.
- There is no clear advertising channel. These customers don't browse Amazon for security solutions. They

don't sign up for webinars. They aren't clicking on Instagram ads.

- Trust is the currency of the business. A wealthy individual won't work with just any security firm. They'll only consider companies that come through trusted personal referrals.

WPG doesn't advertise the way other consumer brands do. They don't rely on traditional marketing, influencer endorsements or social media engagement. Their growth depends on relationships, confidentiality and reputation.

Their clients don't come from Facebook ads. They come through personal introductions at exclusive clubs, discreet referrals from existing clients and word-of-mouth within the elite circles they serve.

The Business Implications of Reachability

The identifiability of a niche determines everything about how a business operates.

If your niche is easy to identify and reach:

- Marketing is straightforward. You can use search ads, social media and partnerships with industry influencers to target your customers directly.
- Sales cycles are fast. A pregnant woman needs nutritional support *now*, not three months from now. The urgency makes it easier to convert customers quickly.

- Repeat business is built in. If a customer finds success with one Nutrizoe product, they're likely to buy others, like a moringa soup for pregnancy, anti-nausea mixes and high-nutrition snack bars.

If your niche is hard to identify and reach:

- Referrals matter more than marketing. When direct advertising doesn't work, reputation and personal introductions become the main growth engine.
- Trust takes time to build. Unlike Nutrizoe, where a customer might buy immediately, high-net-worth individuals won't hire a security firm until they've done extensive vetting.
- There may be fewer clients, but much higher value. While Nutrizoe makes money through volume, WPG might only need ten clients per year to be wildly profitable.

Where Does Your Niche Fit?

The key question for any niche business is:

Are my customers easy to find, or will I have to go searching for them?

- If your customers are easily identifiable, you can scale through traditional marketing, digital ads and community-building.
- If your customers are hidden or exclusive, growth comes through personal networks, long-term credibility and high-trust referrals.

Both models work – but they require completely different playbooks. And in the world of niche businesses, knowing *who* your customers are is important.

But knowing how to reach them – that's everything.

The Price of a Niche: Premium, Affordable or Somewhere in Between?

A Richard Mille watch doesn't tell time any better than a Casio. In fact, it probably does a worse job because if absolute precision were the goal, we'd all just use our smartphones. But that's not the point. A Richard Mille is an engineering marvel, a work of art, a statement of identity. It can cost upwards of half a million dollars, not because of what it does, but because of what it represents.

Now, contrast that with a Jitterbug phone, a smartphone designed specifically for seniors. It doesn't boast of a titanium case, tourbillon movement or sapphire crystal. Instead, it strips away unnecessary complexity. There are no confusing apps and endless notifications; the phone has large buttons for easier visibility, a simple menu and an emergency call feature. And because it's been pruned of features that its target customers don't value, it's actually cheaper than a regular smartphone.

Both are niche products. Both dominate their markets. But they sit on opposite ends of the pricing spectrum.

The Art of the Super Premium

At the extreme high end of niche pricing, you have brands like MB&F, BOVET and Richard Mille – watchmakers that don't just sell timepieces, but works of mechanical art. These brands operate in a world where price is not a constraint but a signal. The more expensive, the more desirable.

This is what defines super-premium niche products:

- Scarcity is part of the appeal. Richard Mille doesn't flood the market with thousands of watches. Each piece is produced in limited numbers, ensuring exclusivity.
- Craftsmanship and complexity justify the price. Customers aren't just paying for the watch – they're paying for cutting-edge materials, hand-assembled movements and a level of detail that mass-market brands can't afford to offer.
- Customers want to pay more. In the world of high-end watches, price is a psychological moat. If Richard Mille were to sell a watch for $5,000, it would lose its entire appeal. The target audience doesn't want affordable luxury – they want unattainable luxury.

For businesses playing in this space, pricing is not about cost-plus margins. It's about storytelling. The higher the price, the more mythical the brand becomes.

The Power of Pruning: The Affordable Niche

But not every niche business thrives by going ultra-premium. Some win by doing the exact opposite – stripping products down to their core and making them more affordable than the mainstream alternatives.

The Jitterbug phone is an example of how a niche product can be priced lower than its mainstream equivalent. The typical smartphone is a Swiss Army knife of technology – packed with features, right from high-resolution cameras to AI-powered assistants. But if you're a senior citizen who just wants to make calls, send texts and maybe browse the internet, why pay for all the extras?

Jitterbug succeeds not by adding more, but by removing what doesn't matter.

This is what defines affordable niche products:

- They eliminate costly, unnecessary features. By focusing only on what the niche values, the company cuts out expensive components that don't add value.
- They simplify rather than innovate. Unlike a Richard Mille watch, which pushes the boundaries of technology, Jitterbug succeeds by making something easier to use.
- They expand the market by lowering barriers. A high-end watch appeals to an elite few. A Jitterbug phone opens up a product category to millions of seniors who find mainstream smartphones overwhelming.

Affordable niche businesses often aren't trying to outdo the mainstream market. They're trying to serve customers who are being ignored – and doing so at a price that makes buying the product an easy decision.

The Business Implications of Pricing a Niche Product

Whether a niche product is super-premium or ultra-affordable shapes everything about how the business operates.

If your niche is premium-priced:

- Price is a feature, not a drawback. A Richard Mille watch wouldn't sell as well if it were cheaper. The price itself is a marketing tool.
- Craftsmanship and exclusivity are essential. Customers need to feel that they're getting something that few people in the world can access.
- Marketing is about aspiration, not affordability. The goal isn't to convince everyone to buy – it's to make the right audience *want it more.*

If your niche is affordable:

- Simplicity is the key to cost reduction. The more you can remove unwanted features without a corresponding loss in value, the more profitable the product becomes.
- Mass adoption is the goal. Unlike luxury brands, affordable niche businesses thrive on reaching as

many customers as possible.
- Repeat purchases and brand loyalty matter. A Jitterbug phone isn't a one-time luxury splurge – it's a practical product that seniors recommend to others.

Where Does Your Niche Fit?

Some businesses succeed by going ultra-premium, creating products so exclusive that customers fight for the privilege of owning them. Others win by simplifying a product so effectively that it becomes a necessity for an overlooked audience.

- If you're targeting status-driven customers, your price should be high enough to create exclusivity.
- If you're targeting practical, underserved customers, your price should be low enough to remove barriers to purchase.

Both strategies work – but they require entirely different playbooks.

Because in niche businesses, price isn't just about what the product costs to make. It's about what the customer believes it's worth.

Anatomy of a Niche

A niche is not just a focused market – it's a shape, a structure, a set of constraints and opportunities that define how a business must operate. Some niches are vast but scattered, like products for left-handed people. Others are intensely localized, like dry cleaning Broadway costumes. Certain niches demand technical mastery and R&D investment, like ejection seats. Others thrive on simplicity and clarity, like phones for seniors. Some are easily identifiable, like maternity nutrition, while services like VIP security operate in a world where their customers value discretion. And then there's pricing: some niches command exclusivity through a premium, while others dominate through affordability. Each of these facets – B2B versus B2C, size, geography, reachability, complexity and price – shapes how a niche business is built, how it grows and how it competes. Understanding these dimensions isn't just an academic exercise but a practical guide to making the right strategic choices. Because in the world of niche businesses, success isn't just about finding an underserved market. It's about understanding the nature of that market well enough to serve it better than anyone else ever could.

- Niches come in many shapes – defined not just by size, but by how they operate.
- B2B niches rely on expertise and relationships. B2C niches thrive on branding and emotion.
- **Size**: Some niches are large but globally scattered. Others are tiny with a few high-value customers.
- **Geography Matters**: Some niches are global (like harmonicas), others hyper-local (like Broadway costume cleaning).
- **Complexity Varies**: Some niches demand technical depth; others succeed with simplicity and insight.
- **Reachability Changes Strategy**: Easily identifiable customers need marketing; hard-to-reach ones need trust and referrals.
- **Pricing also Defines Niches**: Some win through premium positioning, others by being stripped-down and affordable.
- The key is understanding the shape of your niche. That shape will determine how you compete and grow.

4

INDIA

LAND OF A MILLION NICHES

In the West, the idea of a niche market is often treated as a modern discovery, a strategic manoeuvre in an era of hyper-competition. In India, however, niches are not a business strategy. They are a way of life.

To understand why India is the ultimate ground for niche businesses, you must first understand India itself – not as a monolithic entity, but as a vast and intricate web of divisions, subcultures and micro-identities. Every few hundred kilometres, languages change, food preferences shift, clothing styles transform and consumer behaviour follows suit. India does not have one market; it has thousands. A sari store in Kanchipuram will sell a very different weave from one in Varanasi. A tea seller in Darjeeling caters to an entirely different clientele than one in Assam. Even something as simple as salt has regional variations, from the pink Himalayan salt of the north to the black salt used in chaat across the country.

India's diversity isn't just cultural – it is functional. Take religion, caste and community. These factors have historically played a significant role in shaping economic activity. A city like Mumbai might seem like one unified metropolis, but it operates as a collection of specialized economic clusters. The Zaveri Bazaar is the epicentre of gold trading, while Dadar is home to Marathi book publishers. Dharavi, often branded as Asia's largest slum, is a powerhouse of micro-industries – from leather goods to pottery – each catering to a distinct market. This fractal-like subdivision ensures that demand is never homogeneous. Instead, businesses in India thrive by serving the hyper-specific needs of clearly defined customer segments.

A Country Built on Specialization

If diversity defines India's market, specialization has defined its economy for centuries. Long before 'niches' became a buzzword, Indian society was structured around the idea of micro-expertise. The caste system, despite its many inequities, also functioned as a system of economic specialization. The weavers of Kanchipuram didn't make pottery, just as the potters of Khurja didn't weave silk. Skills were passed down through generations, refining manufacturing techniques to a level of mastery that made Indian goods highly sought after across the world. This was not just division of labour – it was an institutionalized form of niche excellence.

Even today, this tradition of specialization persists. The town of Moradabad in Uttar Pradesh is synonymous with brass handicrafts. Tamil Nadu's Tirupur is the undisputed hub of India's knitwear industry. Gujarat's Surat dominates the global diamond-cutting market, polishing over 90 per cent of the world's diamonds. These are not just industries; they are entire ecosystems built around a singular focus. In a world where businesses are often encouraged to expand horizontally, Indian enterprises have historically succeeded by going deep rather than wide.

This cultural predisposition toward specialization makes India a fertile ground for niche businesses. A start-up in the US might struggle to build a customer base around an extremely specific product. In India, even the most specialized markets can be vast. A brand catering solely to left-handed people in the US might seem eccentric; in India, even if just 1 per cent of the population falls into that category, that's a potential market of 14 million people.

For entrepreneurs, this presents an extraordinary opportunity. India is not a country where one-size-fits-all solutions thrive. It is a country where success belongs to those who understand the power of specificity. Whether it's a D2C Ayurvedic skincare brand tailored to South India's humidity or an e-commerce platform focused exclusively on Bengali sweets, businesses that embrace India's infinite niches don't just find a market – they create a world of their own.

The Scale of Small

Big numbers are seductive. The start-up world loves the billion-dollar valuation, the hockey-stick growth curve, the promise of scale that transforms a garage project into a behemoth. But in India, the most fascinating businesses often operate in the opposite direction – not despite scale, but because of it.

In the chaos of Covid, when board exams were postponed and most students found themselves adrift, Ananya Malhotra, a school student in Delhi, saw an opening. The internet was already flooded with new clothing brands, dozens launching every day, many waving the now-familiar flag of sustainability. But Ananya wasn't interested in blending in. She spotted something others overlooked: a micro-trend in crochet fashion.

Crochet had all the right ingredients: handmade, nostalgic, slow fashion at its core. And because no major brand had fully tapped into it, she saw an opportunity to carve out a niche. So, while her peers were anxiously refreshing websites for revised exam schedules, she launched Enchanted Threads, a brand devoted entirely to sustainable crochet clothing.

The narrow focus paid off. Her designs stood out, and early traction followed. By 2025, she had built a loyal Instagram following of 30,000, turned her venture into a livelihood for thirty women artisans and managed it all while pursuing a mathematics degree at Delhi University.

Most entrepreneurs start with a grand vision. Ananya started with a stitch, a single thread woven into an idea. And in doing so, she proved that sometimes, the smallest niches hold the biggest opportunities.

Consider the case of the ₹1,200-crore brand, Nalli Silks, one of India's most iconic sari retailers. In an era when fast fashion and mass production dictate global retail, Nalli thrives by doing exactly what it has always done: selling handcrafted, region-specific saris with a level of authenticity and expertise that no generalist brand can match. It doesn't need to be everything to everyone. It only needs to be the best at what it does.

In India, small is not a limitation; it is a strategy. With over 1.4 billion people, even the narrowest slice of the market can translate into millions of customers. A business that caters only to Tamil Brahmins' wedding rituals, or Gujarati Jain food preferences or Assamese silk weaves, can build a loyal customer base without ever having to expand beyond its niche. The sheer density of cultural and regional specificity in India makes specialization not just viable but necessary.

And yet, conventional business wisdom often

overlooks this. Investors, particularly those trained in Western markets, ask about scale before they ask about sustainability. They assume that the endgame of every business should be national or even global expansion. But India's most successful niche businesses don't scale by stretching horizontally; they scale by going deeper. They expand their expertise, build unshakable brand loyalty and become irreplaceable within their chosen market.

Where Big Players Fear to Tread

For all their resources, big companies often struggle in India's fragmented market. They rely on efficiency, standardization and economies of scale – three things that do not always align with the country's intricate consumer landscape. This creates vast pockets of opportunity where large corporations hesitate to go, and where smaller, more agile players can thrive.

Take the case of Patanjali, the Ayurvedic consumer goods company. When Baba Ramdev launched Patanjali, multinational giants like Unilever and Colgate-Palmolive dominated the personal care and fast-moving consumer goods (FMCG) sector in India. But they were playing a different game – one based on mass appeal and global formulations. Patanjali, on the other hand, understood the deep-rooted cultural affinity for Ayurveda in India. It built its brand not on advertising blitzes, but on trust, tradition and a deep connection to the spiritual and health-conscious Indian consumer. The result? A business that grew from an afterthought to achieving a ₹9,000-crore turnover in the 2022 fiscal year by focusing on a niche market that the big players underestimated.

The same pattern repeats across industries. Large food delivery platforms like Zomato and Swiggy operate on a model that prioritizes major urban centres and mainstream restaurant chains. But in cities like Indore, smaller competitors thrive by catering to hyper-local preferences – delivering home-made meals from neighbourhood kitchens or focusing exclusively on regional delicacies that aren't profitable for national players to handle.

In India, the path to success is not always about competing with the giants on their terms. It's about finding the spaces they ignore, the complexities they find too messy to navigate, the customers they overlook. The most powerful opportunities often lie not in the centre of the market, but in the margins.

For the Indian entrepreneur, this is the great advantage: the ability to build something meaningful not by chasing scale, but by mastering the art of small. In a country that thrives on specificity, the businesses that win are the ones that understand that scale isn't just about being big – it's about being irreplaceable in the right place.

Inside the Niche

Somewhere in the small town of Firozabad, Uttar Pradesh, a man sits in a workshop, watching the flames dance at the mouth of an ablaze furnace. This is the heart of India's glass bangle industry, a centuries-old craft where artisans blow, mould and fuse molten glass into delicate rings that adorn the wrists of millions of women across the country. The bangle makers work with an instinctive precision, knowing exactly how to shape the glass before it cools and when to apply the right pressure.

A few years ago, an entrepreneur from Delhi visited Firozabad, fascinated by the industry's legacy. He wanted to modernize the business, bring in mechanization, scale up production and sell bangles online to a younger audience. On paper, it made perfect sense. The market was massive, the demand was stable and the margins were healthy. But the plan collapsed almost as soon as it started. The traditional artisans rejected the machines outright – they were built for efficiency, but not for the subtle craftsmanship Firozabad's heritage craft required. The designs failed to resonate with buyers, who valued bangles not just as accessories but as cultural artefacts, carrying personal and regional significance. The entrepreneur had approached the niche as a business case, not as a living, breathing ecosystem.

On the other hand, James Joseph didn't just stumble

upon jackfruit flour. He arrived at it the way all great niche entrepreneurs do – by connecting the dots between culture, science and an unmet need.

For years, Joseph had lived in the world of technology, working at Microsoft and far removed from the food industry. But as a Malayali, he had an instinctive understanding of Kerala's innate love for jackfruit. It wasn't just a fruit; it was a staple, a tradition, a nostalgia-laden symbol of home. Yet, as much as Malayalis loved jackfruit, few saw it as a serious solution to a pressing health crisis – diabetes, which affected nearly one in five adults in the state.

Joseph began digging deeper. He reached out to diabetics, not just to understand their struggles but to gauge their openness to trying something unconventional. He consulted friends in the food and FMCG industries, absorbing everything from supply chain logistics to consumer psychology. And then, he did something that most entrepreneurs in India rarely do – he backed his product with rigorous science. A randomized, double-blind, placebo-controlled study confirmed that 30 grams of green jackfruit flour a day, replacing an equal volume of rice or atta, significantly reduced blood sugar levels and HbA1c counts within three months.

Armed with both cultural intuition and clinical validation, he launched Jackfruit365, India's first green jackfruit flour for diabetics. It was a simple but transformative idea: take something deeply familiar to a region and reintroduce it in a way that solves a modern problem.

This wasn't just a product launch. It was a masterclass in how niche businesses are built – by starting with an insight that others have overlooked, embedding oneself in the world of the customer and methodically bridging the gap between tradition and innovation.

This is the central truth about niche markets: you cannot truly serve them unless you embed yourself completely within them.

The Illusion of Understanding

The mistake many entrepreneurs make is believing they can understand a niche from the outside. They run surveys, analyse data, scan industry reports, maybe even speak to a few potential customers. But niches – especially the most enduring and profitable ones – are built on subcultures, habits and histories that outsiders don't immediately see.

Consider the world of performance cycling. Rapha, the premium bicycle brand, became a global cult phenomenon not just because they made high-quality gear, but because they immersed themselves in the culture of serious cyclists. Their marketing didn't rely on flashy advertisements – it was woven into long-form storytelling, celebrating the grit, suffering and camaraderie of the sport. They didn't just sell jerseys and bib shorts; they sold an identity, a solid understanding of what it meant to be a serious cyclist.

Or take the case of Sugar Cosmetics in India. When Vineeta Singh started the brand, she wasn't just launching another line of lipsticks. She spent years struggling to find make-up that suited her Indian skin tone and withstood the country's humidity, and she discovered that many Indian women have the same pain. The brand's formulations, shade range and messaging weren't dictated by global trends – they were shaped by the everyday needs and frustrations faced by Indian consumers. Today, Sugar competes with global giants, but it succeeded because it understood the niche from the inside out.

Listening Versus Living

The difference between a successful niche brand and a failed one is often the difference between listening to the niche and living in it. When Patagonia first started making outdoor gear, Yvon Chouinard wasn't just a businessman – he was a rock climber who built equipment because he needed it himself. The company's deep environmental ethos didn't come from focus groups. Instead, it emerged from the lived experience of climbers, surfers and hikers who saw first-hand the destruction of nature.

On the other hand, look at the countless 'luxury ayurvedic' brands that have flooded the Indian market in recent years. Many of them saw Ayurveda as an aesthetic – an opportunity to slap Sanskrit names onto packaging and charge a premium for their product. But true ayurvedic customers don't just want expensive serums; they want authenticity. Kama Ayurveda, for example, succeeded not by following trends, but by embedding itself in the philosophy of pure formulations, traditional methods and partnerships with authentic ayurvedic institutions.

Becoming One with the Niche

India is a big opportunity, but not an easy one. To be successful, one needs to be completely in sync with your niche. So how does one truly understand a niche? The answer isn't in analytics – it's in immersion.

- Spend time in the spaces where your niche exists. If you want to build a business around artisanal coffee, don't just read reports on the coffee market. Spend weeks with baristas, roasters and growers. If you're launching a fitness brand, train with athletes, join their communities, understand what they really need.
- Observe the rituals, not just the transactions. Great niche businesses aren't just about selling a product; they're about serving a deeper habit, need or identity. The best tea brands in India don't just sell loose leaves – they understand the rituals around chai drinking

and the differences between Assam, Darjeeling and masala chai enthusiasts.
- Talk less, listen more. The best niche entrepreneurs rarely start by assuming they know what's best. They embed themselves in the niche, listen to frustrations, observe behaviours and let their customers tell them what needs to be built.

The Niche Decides

In the end, the niche decides who belongs. It welcomes those who respect its culture, take the time to understand its nuances and become part of its world. It rejects those who treat it as an opportunity rather than a community.

A niche is not a market segment to be exploited. It is a subculture to be understood. And the only way to build something lasting within it is to step inside, listen, observe and let the niche reveal itself to you.

The Loyalty Factor: Trust Rules the Market

In India, trust isn't just an advantage – it's the currency of business. More so in niche markets, where customers aren't just looking for a product; they're looking for reliability, familiarity and a sense of belonging.

Walk into a neighbourhood kirana store, and you'll notice something remarkable. Customers don't just buy groceries; they have conversations. They ask for recommendations. They tell the shopkeeper to 'put it on the tab', well aware that their balance will be remembered, sometimes without a ledger. This isn't just a relic of old-world commerce – it's a fundamental truth of Indian consumer behaviour. Trust, once built, is rarely broken.

Nowhere is this more evident than in niche businesses. A particular Bengali sweet shop in Delhi will have customers who return not just because of taste but because of the assurance that the sweets are made the traditional way, with ingredients sourced from Kolkata. A family jeweller in Chennai will serve multiple generations, not because his gold is any shinier, but because his word is as good as a certificate of authenticity. In India, loyalty isn't transactional – it's personal.

For start-ups, this is both an opportunity and a challenge. A mass-market brand can grow on the back of aggressive pricing and advertising. A niche business, however, thrives on reputation. In a country where word-of-mouth is still the most powerful marketing tool, a single bad experience can spread faster than any ad campaign. But the flip side is equally true – a business that earns trust doesn't just gain customers; it gains advocates, defenders and lifelong patrons.

In the West, companies talk about customer retention in percentages. In India, it's measured in generations.

- **India Is Inherently Fragmented**: With immense cultural, regional, linguistic and community diversity, India isn't one market – it's thousands of micro-markets.
- **Specialization Is in India's DNA**: From traditional caste-based crafts to regional industrial hubs like Surat (diamonds) and Tirupur (knitwear), India thrives on deep, generational expertise.
- **Small Is Big**: Even hyper-specific niches – like Tamil wedding rituals or crochet fashion – can translate into millions of customers, given India's population scale.
- **Where Giants Hesitate, Niche Brands Thrive**: Large companies often ignore complex, fragmented needs. Indian entrepreneurs succeed by going deep, not wide.
- **Niches Require Immersion**: Successful businesses don't just analyse the niche – they live in it. From Jackfruit365 to Sugar Cosmetics, insider understanding is key.
- **Trust Is Everything**: In niche markets, loyalty is personal. Indian consumers value relationships, word-of-mouth and legacy over flash and scale.

5

HUNTING THE UNSEEN

HOW TO SPOT THE PERFECT NICHE

Most great business ideas don't announce themselves – they aren't the neon-lit, high-traffic intersections of commerce. Instead, they exist in the overlooked alleyways, the spaces between the obvious opportunities – the places where big companies don't think to look. Finding a niche is an act of pattern recognition: a way of seeing what others dismiss as too small, too specific or too unconventional. It requires looking at the world through a different lens, recognizing that where there is frustration, neglect or deep passion, there is also untapped demand.

Finding Hidden Markets

There are patterns to how niche markets emerge. Over time, entrepreneurs have developed different ways of spotting them – frameworks that act as mental models for identifying business opportunities where others see nothing. These frameworks overlap, often blending into one another, but each offers a distinct way of thinking about where new markets can be found.

1. The Unmet Needs Approach: Start with a Problem

The simplest and most powerful way to find a niche is to look for a problem that isn't being solved well. Not just any problem, but one that is specific, persistent and frustrating enough that people would be willing to pay for a better solution. The best businesses don't create demand; they meet demand that already exists but isn't being adequately served.

Consider Mamaearth, an Indian skincare brand that recognized a major gap: parents who wanted toxin-free, natural skincare products for their babies had few reliable options. The problem wasn't that natural skincare didn't exist. But mainstream brands weren't addressing the specific needs of health-conscious millennial parents. By zeroing in on this frustration, Mamaearth built a business that rapidly expanded into a dominant niche.

The key to this approach is listening. Great entrepreneurs don't just observe markets; they listen to complaints and inefficiencies. A niche isn't created – it's uncovered by paying close attention to what people wish existed.

2. The Underserved Communities Approach: Who Is Being Ignored?

Sometimes, a market exists, but a particular group of customers within it is being ignored. They may not fit the generalist mould, or they may be considered too niche to serve profitably by larger companies. But what big businesses see as too small, niche entrepreneurs see as an opportunity.

Think of BharatAgri, an agri-tech start-up in India. Most technology start-ups chase urban consumers, assuming that rural farmers are too disconnected or difficult to serve. But BharatAgri recognized that tech-savvy small Indian farmers were hungry for knowledge on improving their yields and managing unpredictable weather. By creating an app tailored to their specific needs, BharatAgri tapped into a massive but underserved community – one that traditional agribusiness giants had largely ignored.

The challenge with this approach is understanding the overlooked customer. Large corporations struggle in this domain because they build for the *average* user. Niche businesses thrive because they build for the *specific* user.

3. The Emerging Trends Approach: Seeing the Future before Others Do

Some niches exist not because they were ignored by larger brands, but because they are only just beginning to take shape. Identifying these opportunities requires spotting cultural, technological or lifestyle shifts before they become mainstream.

A great example is the explosion of vegan and plant-based foods in India. While vegetarianism is common in India, veganism was virtually unheard of outside of a small group of health-conscious consumers. But as global health trends and ethical concerns around animal products gained traction, the demand for plant-based foods surged. In 2023, the plant-based meat market in India was valued at $78.6 million. Mordor Intelligence estimates the meat substitutes market will reach $737.2 million by 2030. Brands like GoodDot, which specializes in plant-based meat alternatives, saw this shift early and positioned themselves as leaders before the market caught up. Incidentally, GoodDot started in Jaipur, the capital city of the largely vegetarian Rajasthan.

The best way to capitalize on emerging trends is to pay attention to what's happening at the edges – in small subcultures, online communities and experimental product categories. By the time a trend is mainstream, it's too late to own the niche. The opportunity belongs to those who get there first.

4. The Specialized Skills and Interests Approach: Passion as a Business Model

Some of the most defensible niches are built around specialized skills, hobbies or deep interests. These markets may be small, but they are often filled with passionate customers who are willing to spend significantly more than the average consumer.

Take the rise of professional gaming accessories in India. For years, gaming was seen as a casual hobby, but a growing electronic sports (esports) industry created a new kind of customer: competitive gamers who needed high-performance keyboards, mice and chairs. Brands like Cosmic Byte and Zebronics made the most of this trend by creating specialized products that catered specifically to Indian gamers.

Niche businesses that cater to hobbyists and professionals don't need massive customer bases; they need high-value customers who care deeply about their purchases. Passion-driven markets tend to be small but extremely loyal.

5. The Geographic Niche Approach: Serving the Localized Need

As we had discussed in the previous chapter, India is not one market but a collection of thousands of micro-markets. What works in Mumbai may not work in Manipur. What succeeds in Bengaluru may fail in Bhopal. Understanding this is key to unlocking niche opportunities.

Consider the rise of the Haryanvi OTT platform, Stage. While Netflix and Amazon Prime chased the pan-Indian market, Stage, starting with Haryanvi, focused on hyper-local content, recognizing that regional audiences had distinct tastes that mainstream streaming services weren't serving well.

This approach works particularly well in a country as diverse as India, where linguistic, climatic and cultural variations create an almost endless supply of localized niche markets. Stage has over 1.2 million paying subscribers in Haryana alone, and is adding 2,50,000 new subscribers every month.

6. The Value-Based Niche Approach: When Beliefs Drive Purchasing Decisions

Consumers are no longer just buying products – they are buying into values. Sustainability, ethical sourcing and social responsibility have become powerful motivators for niche businesses.

Take Bare Necessities, a brand that creates zero-waste personal care and home products in India. While conventional FMCG companies continued producing plastic-heavy packaging, Bare Necessities built an entire business around eco-conscious consumers willing to pay a premium for sustainable alternatives.

The key to value-based niches is authenticity. Customers in these markets are highly sceptical of shallow marketing tactics, such as greenwashing. To succeed, businesses must *truly* embody the values they promote.

7. The Price-Based Niche Approach: High-End or Low-End, but Never in the Middle

Markets often cluster around the middle – products and services designed for the average consumer. But niche businesses can thrive by positioning themselves at the extreme ends of the pricing spectrum.

Luxury niches, like customized jewellery brands in Jaipur, serve high-net-worth individuals who want exclusivity and craftsmanship. On the other hand, budget niches, like affordable co-living spaces for students, cater to those who prioritize price over brand names.

The mistake many businesses make is trying to please everyone. Niche pricing works because it forces clarity – either serve the high-end with unmatched quality or dominate the low-end with unbeatable affordability.

8. The Hybrid Niche Approach: Where the Real Magic Happens

The most powerful niches often emerge at the intersection of multiple frameworks. The more specific the niche, the harder it is for competitors to replicate.

Consider a brand that combines sustainability (a value-based niche) with plus-size fashion (an underserved community) and localized Indian designs (a geographic niche). That's not just a niche – that's a fortress.

The best niche businesses don't just find one angle. They layer multiple angles to create something that feels truly one of a kind.

Niches are everywhere. They exist across problems, underserved communities, emerging trends, passions, geographies, values, price extremes and the unexpected combinations of these elements. The challenge isn't whether a niche exists – it's whether you can see it before others do.

Niche Hunting in the Digital Age: How the Internet Became a Treasure Map

In 2004, a frustrated mother in New York took to an internet forum to vent. She had spent hours searching for a stylish, durable and chemical-free lunchbox for her kids, but everything on the market was either flimsy, ugly or made of materials high in toxins. Within minutes, other parents chimed in. They had the same problem.

It was a small, almost invisible complaint in the grand digital landscape – one of millions of grievances aired online every day. But for an entrepreneur paying attention, it was a goldmine. Within a year, a small company launched a line of stainless steel, bisphenol A (BPA)-free lunchboxes. They sold out almost immediately.

This is how niches are discovered today. They aren't found in boardrooms or focus groups. They don't announce themselves with flashy billboards. Instead, they emerge from the collective murmur of the internet – hidden in product reviews, Twitter rants, Reddit threads and shifting Google search trends. The digital world, chaotic as it may seem, is the ultimate treasure map. The key is knowing where to look.

The Social Media Echo Chamber: Listening Between the Lines

Social media is loud, messy and often absurd. It's where people post vacation selfies and debate whether pineapple belongs on pizza. But underneath all the noise, social media is also the most powerful real-time market research tool ever created.

Take the rise of plant-based meat. Five years before Beyond Meat and Impossible Foods became household names, vegan Twitter was filled with complaints. The problem? Veggie burgers tasted terrible. They were dry, bland and nothing like the real thing. The demand for a realistic meat alternative was there – just waiting for someone to notice.

Platforms like Twitter, Instagram and Reddit serve as a digital pulse check. What are people raving about? What are they complaining about? What trends are bubbling under the surface, just waiting to explode? Tools like Brand24 and Mention allow businesses to track these conversations at scale. It's digital eavesdropping, but for entrepreneurs, it's also an open invitation to monitor specific keywords, trends and sentiment shifts in real time.

Google Trends: The Crystal Ball of Consumer Behaviour

If social media is a pulse check, Google Trends is a telescope into the future. Every day, billions of searches flow through Google, revealing exactly what people are curious about, worried about or desperate to find.

In 2016, searches for 'minimalist wallets' started climbing steadily. For decades, wallets had been bulky leather rectangles stuffed with receipts and loyalty cards. But suddenly, people wanted something slimmer, sleeker – just enough to hold the essentials. A few savvy entrepreneurs noticed the trend early and launched Kickstarter campaigns for slim, radio frequency identification-blocking wallets. They launched Keplero and raised over half a million.

Google Trends doesn't just show what's popular now – it shows where the world is headed. A spike in searches for 'sleep optimization' might suggest an opportunity for better-designed blackout curtains. A steady rise in 'quiet luxury' could mean the next big thing isn't flashy brands, but subtle, understated craftsmanship. The data is there. All it takes is curiosity – and the ability to connect the dots.

Customer Reviews: The Most Honest Focus Group in the World

Nobody is more brutally honest than an unhappy customer. And nowhere do people air their grievances more freely than in product reviews.

In the early days of noise-cancelling headphones, most reviews followed a pattern. People loved the sound quality, but they hated the bulk. The headphones were too big. Too heavy. Uncomfortable for long flights. For years, the market leaders largely ignored these complaints. Then, Nothing, a UK-based startup saw the gap and introduced ultra-lightweight noise-cancelling earbuds. They became a significant player almost overnight.

Review sites, app stores and e-commerce platforms like Amazon are filled with these breadcrumbs. Look for the patterns:

- What complaints keep coming up again and again?
- What do customers wish a product could do – but doesn't?
- What features are they willing to pay more for?

Each of these frustrations is a potential business waiting to happen.

The Goldmine of Online Communities

Somewhere on the internet, there is a forum dedicated to the exact problem you're trying to solve.

In 2012, a small company stumbled across a niche subreddit filled with people passionate about mechanical keyboards. These users weren't satisfied with mass-market keyboards. They wanted specific switch types, customizable keycaps and better build quality. But no major brand was catering to them. Within a few years, the mechanical keyboard industry exploded – driven almost entirely by these enthusiasts.

From Facebook groups to niche subreddits to Discord communities, the internet is filled with hyper-engaged audiences discussing their frustrations and desires in real-time. Unlike broad social media platforms, these communities are focused, passionate and deeply invested. A single post asking, 'What's the one product you wish existed?' can yield a dozen business ideas.

Finding a niche in the digital age isn't about guessing. It's about listening. Somewhere online, right now, people are expressing their frustrations. They're looking for solutions that don't exist yet. They're telling you exactly what they want.

The companies that win aren't necessarily the ones with the best ideas. They're the ones paying the most attention.

Digging for Gold: How Keyword Research Unearths Hidden Niche Markets

In 1848, a carpenter named James Marshall discovered gold flakes in the American River in California.

Within months, the world caught wind of the news, and thousands of prospectors descended on the region, hoping to strike it rich. But the ones who truly profited from the gold rush weren't the men blindly digging up dirt – they were the ones who knew *where* to dig.

Finding a niche in the digital age is a lot like that. The internet is an endless landscape filled with opportunities. But if you don't know where to look, you'll waste time sifting through worthless gravel. The key is to stop guessing and start mining with the right tools – Google Keyword Planner, Ahrefs and SEMrush. These function like digital metal detectors, capable of uncovering valuable pockets of demand hidden beneath the surface of broad and obvious markets.

And just like the smartest gold prospectors in history, the most successful businesses aren't the ones searching for 'gold'. They're the ones looking for *exactly* the right kind of gold, in exactly the right place.

Beyond the Obvious: The Power of Long-Tail Keywords

In the early days of search engines, if someone wanted to buy shoes online, they'd type 'shoes' into Google. That's it. One word. The results? An ocean of generic listings from giant brands, all competing for attention.

But that's not how people search anymore. Today, someone looking for shoes isn't just searching for *shoes*. They're searching for:

- ‘best walking shoes for senior citizens with knee pain’
- ‘vegan leather formal shoes for men in India’
- ‘extra-wide running shoes for women size 9’

These are called long-tail keywords, and they are the secret to uncovering profitable niches. They may not have the massive search volume of a generic keyword like ‘shoes’, but what they lack in quantity, they make up for in quality. Someone searching for ‘best walking shoes for senior citizens with knee pain’ isn’t casually browsing. They have a specific problem, they know exactly what they need and they are ready to buy.

For a business, that kind of precision is invaluable.

In India, long-tail keywords reveal some of the most interesting business opportunities. The broader market for ‘saris’ is impossibly competitive – dominated by e-commerce giants, fashion houses and established retailers. But a smart entrepreneur, armed with keyword research, isn’t looking at just ‘saris’. They’re looking at:

- ‘handloom silk saris for wedding guests in Bengaluru’
- ‘affordable cotton saris for daily wear online’
- ‘lightweight saris for hot and humid weather’

Each of these searches reveals not just a product category, but a specific customer, with a specific need, who is actively looking for something that isn’t being easily found.

Or take India’s food delivery market. Competing

for 'biryani delivery' is a losing battle against Swiggy and Zomato, not to speak of Biryani Blues, The BVK Biryani, Bikkgane Biryani, Behrouz and Biryani By Kilo. But search data might reveal opportunities in:

- 'vegan biryani delivery near me'
- 'gluten-free biryani catering services in Chennai'
- 'authentic Hyderabadi biryani for large corporate events'

These aren't just search terms. They are maps to underserved markets.

The same principles apply worldwide. Businesses that succeed in niche markets aren't trying to sell clothes. They're selling sustainable plus-size activewear for women over fifty. They aren't just making baby clothes. They're making organic cotton baby clothes for premature infants.

A tech company isn't launching another project management tool. It's creating 'workflow automation software for freelance graphic designers' – because long-tail search data told them that people were already looking for it.

Mining for Opportunity: How Keyword Tools Work

The good news is that, unlike the gold rush of the 1800s, today's entrepreneurs don't need a pickaxe or head to a riverbed to find opportunities. They just need the right tools:

- **Google Keyword Planner**: Lets you enter a basic product idea and discover related searches, along with their search volume and competition level.
- **Ahrefs**: Helps you analyse what keywords competitors are ranking for, revealing gaps in the market.
- **SEMrush**: Provides insights into trending keywords and long-tail search terms that could signal an emerging niche.

But raw data isn't enough. The real value comes from understanding the intent behind the searches.

Who are people searching for 'best yoga mats for travel', and why? Are they backpackers looking for something lightweight? Are they business travellers trying to maintain a fitness routine? Are they senior citizens looking for something easy to roll up and store?

Each of these nuances points to a different product, a different message and a different market strategy.

Keyword research isn't just about search volume or rankings. It's about uncovering what people really want, and then creating something so perfectly suited to their needs that competition becomes irrelevant.

The businesses that thrive in the digital age aren't the ones shouting the loudest. They're the ones listening the hardest.

The Lost Art of Seeing: Finding Niches the Old-Fashioned Way

In 1965, a man named Karsanbhai Patel would finish his shift at his government job in Gujarat, come home and start mixing detergent powder in his backyard. At the time, detergent was a luxury in India – something imported, expensive and out of reach for most middle-class households. Patel noticed something that multinational companies had missed: people wanted clean clothes, but they didn't want to pay a premium for them.

So, he started selling his home-made detergent, Nirma, door to door on his bicycle. It was cheaper than anything on the market, and it worked just as well. Within a decade, Nirma had completely disrupted the detergent industry, forcing giants like Unilever to scramble for a response.

Patel didn't conduct a survey. He didn't run focus groups or hire a market research firm. He simply *paid attention*.

Before algorithms and analytics, Google Trends and social media monitoring, entrepreneurs found business ideas by observing people – watching how they lived, what they struggled with and what they quietly wished existed. The world has changed since Patel's time, but the fundamental skill of *seeing* remains as powerful as ever.

The Power of Personal Observation

The most valuable insights aren't found in spreadsheets. They're found in everyday moments – someone improvising a solution, struggling with an inconvenience or unknowingly revealing an unmet need.

Howard Schultz, the man who turned Starbucks into a global phenomenon, didn't get the idea from a report on the coffee industry. He got it by *watching* how Italians treated coffee. During a trip to Milan, he noticed that cafés weren't just places to grab a quick espresso – they were social hubs, part of the fabric of daily life. He realized that Americans had coffee, but they didn't have a coffee culture. Starbucks wasn't just built on selling coffee. It was built on bringing the Italian café experience to the US.

Closer to home, Chumbak – the quirky India-inspired lifestyle brand – was born when its founders, Shubhra Chadda and Vivek Prabhakar, noticed something missing from Indian souvenir shops. Every time tourists visited India, they bought brass idols and carved elephants, but nothing modern and colourful that truly reflected contemporary India. That simple realization led to a brand that now sells everything from phone cases to home decor, all infused with a uniquely Indian aesthetic.

The lesson? You don't always need data to spot an opportunity. Sometimes, all you need is to look around.

Talking to People: The Most Underrated Market Research Tool

Some of the best market research comes from simply having conversations.

Ritesh Agarwal, the founder of OYO Rooms, was just eighteen when he started travelling across India on a budget. He spent nights in small hotels and guest houses, and one thing became painfully obvious: the budget hotel experience was terrible. No standardization, no guarantees and no trust. He didn't read about this in a market report – he lived it. And when he started asking other travellers about their experiences, he realized he wasn't alone. That insight became the foundation for OYO's model of branding and standardizing budget hotels.

Traditional businesses relied on these kinds of insights long before technology took over. Store owners would chat with customers, salespeople would hear about problems first-hand and traders in old bazaars would adjust their offerings based on what people asked for the most. The best entrepreneurs still do this today.

- **Surveys and Focus Groups**: While not as organic as casual observation, structured conversations can reveal deep insights. Asking potential customers directly about their frustrations and preferences often uncovers opportunities no competitor has noticed.
- **One-on-One Interviews**: Instead of guessing what

people want, talking to them in depth about their challenges often leads to breakthrough ideas.

- **Watching Competitors Closely**: If a product is doing well but has a consistent flaw that customers complain about, that's an opportunity. A new business doesn't need to reinvent the wheel – it just needs to make the wheel run smoother.

Finding the Gaps That Big Companies Ignore

Large corporations rely on structured, data-driven research. They track trends at scale, but that very scale often makes them blind to smaller, specific opportunities.

Darshan Patel noticed that cracked heels were a persistent problem troubling many Indians, and none of the FMCG or pharmaceutical majors had a product for that problem. He also realized that the ones facing this problem the most were housewives who worked barefoot in damp spaces like kitchens and washing areas. He leveraged the regional ayurvedic solutions to come up with Krack Cream in 1993, which dominated this niche market for the next three decades.

Similarly, Lahori wasn't built by analysing beverage industry trends. Its founders realized that despite the dominance of colas and packaged fruit juices, people still craved traditional Indian drinks – Zeera, Shikanji, Imli Banta. Their demand outstripped availability. Lahori didn't create a new category; it simply filled a cultural gap.

The Best Niches Aren't Always Found Online

Today, businesses rely heavily on digital tools to spot opportunities, but the best niche ideas often start offline.

Think about the mother who spends hours altering mass-market baby clothes because they don't fit premature infants properly. The shopkeeper who always runs out of a certain type of spice because people keep asking for it. The street vendor who sells out of one item by noon, while the others stay untouched.

These are the signals. The clues. The real-world indicators of demand.

Technology makes research easier, but the entrepreneurs who win are the ones who know how to *see* – to recognize frustrations, listen to unspoken desires and notice what everyone else has learned to ignore.

Because at the end of the day, the best niche isn't something you search for. It's something you *realize*.

- Niches hide in plain sight, existing in unmet needs, frustrations and overlooked communities.
- There are eight frameworks to spot a niche:
  1. **Unmet Needs**: Solve specific problems people already care about.
  2. **Underserved Communities**: Focus on groups ignored by big players.

3. **Emerging Trends**: Catch cultural or tech shifts early.
4. **Specialized Skills or Passions**: Serve enthusiasts and professionals.
5. **Geographic Niches**: Localize for India's micro-markets.
6. **Value-Based Niches**: Align with ethical or lifestyle beliefs.
7. **Price Extremes**: Go ultra-premium or ultra-affordable, never average.
8. **Hybrid Niches**: Combine multiple angles for a unique edge.

- Digital tools like Google Trends, keyword research and social media monitoring now act as real-time maps for discovering niche demand.
- Offline observation still matters. This encompasses talking to users, noticing behaviours and living within a niche reveals insights data often misses.
- Great niche businesses don't chase trends. They listen deeply, embed themselves in the culture and build from within.

6

THE RIGHT BET

CHOOSING A NICHE THAT WORKS

Cartken started with a niche idea in the autonomous electric vehicle (EV) space: tiny sidewalk robots delivering food. Burritos, sushi, pizza – all rolled out with precision. But co-founder Christian Bersch always saw more. The real opportunity wasn't just food delivery; it was movement – seamless, uninterrupted navigation between sidewalks, factories and even airports.

That's a much harder problem than it sounds. Most autonomous robots work either indoors or outdoors. Cartken's breakthrough was building a system that did both. Their AI-driven, camera-based robots – no light detection and ranging (LiDAR), no GPS – could navigate unpredictable environments. They braved the sun, rain, potholes and pedestrians without missing a beat. Investors took notice, pouring in $22.5 million.

Cartken's bots now crisscross college campuses in Miami, Virginia and Tokyo, handling 36,000 deliveries a month with Uber Eats and Grubhub. But their next frontier isn't food – it's industry. At a German auto plant, the robots have replaced bicycle couriers, shuttling parts across vast factory floors. In labs and factories, they've saved workers 10,000 hours in a year.

The demand, Bersch says, has been surprising. Companies had searched for a hybrid indoor–outdoor solution and found nothing. Until now. Cartken isn't just another delivery bot. It hopes to be a blueprint for the future of autonomous movement.

Picking a niche isn't about spotting a random opportunity. It's about choosing the right one – one that matches your skills, aligns with demand and is built to last. The question is: *how do you know when you've found the right niche?*

The Niche Selection Framework: The Three-Fit Test

Zeroing down on a niche isn't simply based on picking what's trendy. The right one strikes the perfect balance between market fit, founder fit and defensibility, getting all three right.

1. Market Fit: Does the Demand Exist?

Before you commit to a niche, the most important question is: *is there a hungry audience for this?*

Some of the biggest business failures come from

founders who fall in love with an idea but forget to check if anyone actually wants it. Take the Segway – a futuristic self-balancing scooter that was supposed to revolutionize urban transportation. The problem? No one *needed* it. It was expensive, impractical and tried to solve a problem that didn't exist. Segway tried B2C markets and then shifted to B2B markets by focusing on the postal department, golf clubs and tour operators. None of these worked.

The best niche businesses start by identifying *real* demand.

Here's how to assess market fit:

- Is the problem urgent? People pay for solutions to problems they feel deeply. If it's just a mild inconvenience, it won't drive sales.
- Are people already spending money in this space? If customers are finding ways to work around a problem – do-it-yourself (DIY) solutions, expensive custom fixes – it's a sign of strong demand.
- Are they complaining online? If people are frustrated enough to post about a problem on social media, forums or reviews, they are *looking* for a solution.

2. Founder Fit: Are You the Right Person for This?

In 2006, Brian Chesky and Joe Gebbia were struggling to pay their rent in San Francisco. When a big design conference came to town and hotels sold out, they saw an opportunity. They set up a simple website offering their apartment as an affordable stay. It worked. That one experiment became Airbnb.

What made Airbnb succeed wasn't just the idea – it was *who* was behind it. Chesky and Gebbia were designers. They understood how to create an experience that felt personal, warm and inviting – something hotels couldn't offer.

When Rachana Gupta speaks about women's health, it isn't from a slide deck or a market report. It comes from the memory of sitting in countless doctor's offices, being told that her gynaecological problems had no real solution. In that frustration lay the seed of Gynoveda. She turned, almost instinctively, to Ayurveda, not as an entrepreneur chasing a trend, but as a woman searching for relief. When the remedies worked, the experience didn't just heal her; it reframed how she thought about an entire category of women silently enduring the same struggles. And that is where her husband, Sandeep, an IIM alum with prior experience of consumer businesses, entered the picture. Together, they transformed a deeply personal journey into a business proposition. The founder fit here is unmistakable: lived experience gave Rachana empathy and authenticity, while Sandeep supplied the strategic scaffolding to scale that insight into a femtech platform that could speak to millions.

A niche business isn't just about the market. It's about *you*. Do you have the passion, skills and insider knowledge to make it work?

Here's how to assess founder fit:

- Do you understand the audience? The best niches come from lived experiences – things you *know* deeply rather than things you just read about.
- Do you care about it enough? Niches require endurance. If you don't care about the space, you won't last when things get hard.
- Do you have a natural advantage? Industry expertise, a strong network or unique skills can make execution easier.

3. Defensibility: Can You Hold Your Ground?

The moment a niche proves to be profitable, competition arrives. The key isn't just finding a niche – it's choosing one that has natural barriers that protect you from bigger players.

Consider Lenskart, India's largest online eyewear brand. When it launched, eyewear in India was still an offline business. Lenskart's competitors could have copied its model, but they didn't have the same logistics, supply chain and customer trust that it had spent years building. That defensibility made all the difference.

Here's how to assess defensibility:

- Is there a moat? Can you create something that's hard to copy – either because of technology, brand loyalty or operational complexity?
- Will customers stay loyal? If your niche is built around deep customer relationships (like Harley-Davidson's cult following), you have built-in protection.

- Does scale work in your favour? Niches that require deep specialization (like handwoven Kanchipuram saris) are harder for mass-market players to disrupt.

Bringing It Together: The Sweet Spot

The best niche businesses find the intersection of market fit, founder fit and defensibility. If a business has just one, it might struggle. If it has two, it might work. But if it has all three? It has the potential to dominate.

Mamaearth, one of India's fastest-growing D2C brands, nailed all three:

- Market fit? Parents were desperate for hazard-free baby care products. The demand was clear.
- Founder fit? The founders, Varun and Ghazal Alagh, were parents themselves, dealing with the same concerns as their customers.
- Defensibility? By focusing on transparency, community-building and the first-mover advantage in toxin-free personal care, Mamaearth created a brand identity that was difficult to replicate.

That's the formula: choosing right beats choosing big.

The biggest mistake entrepreneurs make is thinking that bigger markets mean bigger success. But history has shown time and again that *the right niche beats the biggest market*.

- Starbucks didn't go after generic coffee. It focused on *the café experience*.

- Lenskart didn't try to be a department store. It focused *only* on eyewear.
- Nykaa didn't launch as a general e-commerce site. It built a category leader in *beauty*.

In business, as in life, the best opportunities aren't always the biggest. They're the ones that fit you best.

Testing the Waters: How to Validate a Niche Before You Build

In 2013, before Eric Yuan built Zoom into the $22-billion video conferencing giant that would redefine remote work, he had a different challenge. Yuan had spent years at WebEx, Cisco's leading video conferencing software, and he noticed something troubling – customers weren't happy. Calls dropped, the video lagged and the user experience was clunky. But instead of blindly building yet another conferencing tool, he took a step back.

Before writing a single line of code, Yuan spent months talking to potential users: start-ups, remote workers, global teams. He wanted to understand not just their frustrations, but what an *ideal* solution would look like. He sketched wireframes, presented them to customers and refined the product based on their input. When he finally built Zoom, it wasn't just another video conferencing app – it was precisely what users had been waiting for.

The lesson here is simple. The best niche businesses don't start with a product. They start with proof that the product deserves to exist. And that proof comes before a minimum viable product (MVP – the simplest version of a product that delivers core value to early users), before raising money, before hiring a team.

The Illusion of the MVP Shortcut

The modern start-up playbook tells entrepreneurs to move fast: build an MVP, launch it and iterate based on user feedback. It's an approach that works well when you already know there's demand. But what if you don't? What if you're entering a niche where the market is unproven?

Jumping straight into an MVP can be a costly mistake. Even the simplest version of a product requires design, engineering, marketing and distribution. If you later discover that customers don't actually want it, you've burned through time and resources that could have been spent elsewhere.

That's why pre-validation – testing the core concept before building – is so important. It's the difference between guessing and knowing.

The Art of Niche Pre-Validation

Every niche business is built on two key questions:

1. Does this solve a real problem?
2. Will people actually pay for it?

The goal of pre-validation is to answer both without committing to full-scale product development. There are three key ways to do this: signal testing, audience immersion and competitive benchmarking.

Signal Testing: Throw a Hook into the Market

One of the easiest ways to gauge interest is to put an idea out into the world and see how people respond.

- **Landing Pages and Fake Doors**: Before Dropbox ever existed, its founder, Drew Houston, created a simple landing page explaining the concept. He added a sign-up button, and thousands joined the waitlist. No product, no coding – just a test to see if there was demand. If you're exploring a niche, set up a landing page with an explanation and collect sign-ups. If nobody clicks, you've saved yourself months of wasted effort.
- **Pre-Sales and Waitlists**: Tesla didn't wait until its cars were in production to test demand. Instead, it asked customers to pay for a pre-order before a single car was built. The result? Hundreds of thousands of reservations, proving that there was a market. If people are willing to put money down for something that doesn't exist yet, that's the strongest validation possible.
- **Social Media and Community Response**: If you can't generate excitement within relevant LinkedIn groups, Twitter threads or niche forums, that's a

red flag. A single well-crafted post can give you an early read on whether people are curious about your product.

Audience Immersion: Understand the Customer Before You Build

Pre-validation isn't just about numbers – it's about deeply understanding your audience. When James Joseph started Jackfruit365, he didn't start by immediately manufacturing the flour. Instead, he embedded himself in the world of diabetic patients, nutritionists and healthcare professionals. He spoke to customers, understood their eating habits and refined his approach before going into production.

If you're entering a niche, this kind of immersion is critical. Conduct structured interviews with potential users. Ask them about their current pain points, what alternatives they use and what would make them switch. Many successful niche entrepreneurs start as their first customer. If you're building ultra-light camping gear, go on a long trek and see where current options fail. If you're developing tools for freelance writers, spend a few months working as one. Direct experience often reveals insights that surveys can't.

The Cost of Skipping Pre-Validation

Skipping pre-validation can be disastrous. Some of the biggest start-up failures in history weren't because the product was bad – it was because there was no real demand. Quibi, the short-form streaming service backed by $1.75 billion, assumed people wanted ten-minute high-production videos on their phones. They never tested this assumption. When the product launched, no one cared. It shut down in six months.

Juicero, a start-up that raised $120 million to build an expensive juicing machine, collapsed when people realized they could just squeeze the juice packs by hand. A simple survey or prototype test could have saved investors millions.

Ruplee, a Delhi-based startup, founded in 2014, positioned itself as India's first app to pay restaurant bills digitally. The idea was that you could skip waiting for the bill and pay seamlessly through the app. The reality was that the customers didn't find the 'pain point' to be a real pain point, especially when they could pay using debit or credit cards. Finally, when UPI exploded, Ruplee collapsed.

Contrast that with Tesla's pre-order strategy, Jackfruit365's immersion approach or Zoom's pre-product interviews. The best niche businesses don't just launch – they validate first.

The process isn't complicated.

You create signal, measure response.

You talk to real users, listen carefully.

You study competitors, find the gaps.

Before you build, before you launch – test the waters.

Because the best time to find out if your niche is viable isn't after you've built it. It's before you even start.

The Hidden Pitfalls of Picking a Niche: What to Watch Out For

In 2010, a company called Juicero launched with a bold vision: revolutionize the way people consumed fresh juice. The idea seemed brilliant. Instead of messy juicers and sticky countertops, customers would buy Juicero's sleek, Wi-Fi-enabled machine and insert pre-packaged fruit and vegetable pouches. With the press of a button, fresh, cold-pressed juice would pour into their glass.

Investors loved it. The company raised $120 million, its backers including Google Ventures and top Silicon Valley investors. It was hailed as the future of juicing.

Then, the product launched.

Within weeks, people started posting videos online showing that you didn't actually *need* the machine at all. The expensive, proprietary juice packs could be squeezed *by hand* just as easily – no $400-device required. Within two years, Juicero collapsed, and it became a cautionary tale of what happens when you try to sell what your customer doesn't need.

Choosing a niche isn't just about spotting an opportunity – it's about avoiding the hidden traps that can turn a promising idea into a slow-motion disaster.

Here are the most common pitfalls entrepreneurs fall into when selecting a niche and how to sidestep them:

1. The Mirage of Trends: Just Because It's Hot Doesn't Mean It's Sustainable

Remember Clubhouse?

At the height of the pandemic, the invite-only audio chat app became an overnight sensation. Celebrities, CEOs and influencers all flocked to it. For a brief moment, it seemed like the future of social media. Investors rushed in, valuing the company at $4 billion in 2021.

Then, just as quickly, it faded.

Why? Because Clubhouse wasn't built on sustained demand – it was built on hype. As pandemic restrictions eased and people returned to in-person interactions, the novelty wore off. More importantly, established social media giants like Twitter and Facebook copied its core features. Clubhouse lost its uniqueness, and its users drifted away.

The lesson? Trends create temporary spikes in demand, but that doesn't mean they're viable long-term businesses.

- Non-Fungible Tokens (NFTs) were hot – until people realized their speculative nature.
- Fidget spinners were everywhere – until no one cared anymore.
- The metaverse was supposed to be the future – until even Meta started backing away from it.

When evaluating a niche, ask: *is this a real shift in consumer behaviour, or just a passing craze?*

2. *Overestimating Market Size: The Trap of Thinking Too Big or Too Small*

A niche needs to be small enough to dominate but big enough to sustain a business.

Many entrepreneurs make the mistake of going too broad – thinking they can serve everyone and ending up serving no one. But the opposite is just as dangerous: picking a niche so small that there simply aren't enough customers.

Consider the wave of hyper-niche subscription boxes that flooded the market in the 2010s:

- A subscription box just for left-handed people.
- A subscription box just for dog owners who also like punk rock.
- A subscription box for socks, but only ones with food-themed prints.

The problem? While these were fun ideas, the target audience was too small to sustain long-term growth. Many of these companies lasted only a year or two before shutting down.

Before jumping into a niche, ask:

- How many people actually need this?
- How often will they buy it?
- Will I have enough customers to grow, or will I run out after the early adopters?

A niche that's too small isn't a niche. It's a hobby.

3. The Danger of Being Too Niche: The One-Product Problem

Sometimes a niche is too narrow, not because the audience is too small, but because the business has no room to evolve.

In 1995, Autoriders launched a service called 'Limouzine'. They offered white-collar commuters in Mumbai plush thirty-five-seater buses to go from their homes in the suburbs to their offices in Nariman Point and a ride back after the end of the day. It was a premium-priced service, but there were enough takers to fill the buses in the morning and evening. Unfortunately, there were no takers for the service the rest of the time. The buses remained idle for the rest of the day, and that was not good for profitability. The service was set up specifically for the white-collar commuter and did not attract any other set of users. They tried their best to cater to other travellers but could not do so without eroding their appeal to their core customers. The business quickly came to an end.

A great niche business starts narrow but allows for expansion.

- Apple started with computers but expanded into phones, wearables and services.
- Nike started with running shoes but grew into apparel and lifestyle products.

- Wow Skin Science launched Apple Cider Vinegar Shampoo, marketed as sulfate- and paraben-free, in 2014, and has now expanded to a full portfolio of personal care

A niche should be a starting point, not a prison.

4. Ignoring Margins and Business Viability

In the early 2010s, meal delivery start-ups were everywhere. Companies like Sprig, Munchery, Caloriecare and Maple promised healthy, restaurant-quality meals delivered straight to your door. Customers loved it. Investors poured in money.

And then, one by one, they collapsed.

The reason? Terrible margins.

The cost of food, packaging, delivery logistics and customer acquisition was simply too high to make the business profitable. Even with thousands of customers, they were losing money on every meal.

A niche might have demand, but if the margins are razor-thin, it will never be a sustainable business.

Before jumping in, ask:

- Can I price this high enough to make money?
- What are my actual costs per sale?
- Will I be profitable after customer acquisition costs?

If the math doesn't work, the niche isn't worth pursuing.

5. Competing Against Giants Without an Edge

In 2012, a small company called Color launched with $41 million in funding. It was a photo-sharing app, designed to reinvent the way people captured and shared images. Investors were convinced it would disrupt Instagram.

It didn't.

Instagram already owned the photo-sharing niche. Users were familiar with the app, loyal to it and had no reason to switch. Color didn't offer anything dramatically better. Within a year, it was gone.

The biggest mistake in niche selection? Competing against an entrenched giant with no real differentiation.

Don't launch a generic food delivery app when Swiggy and Zomato exist.

Don't try to be a new ride-sharing platform without a clear edge over Uber and Ola.

Don't start a streaming service unless you have a niche that Netflix can't replicate.

A niche is only valuable if big players can't (or won't) crush you.

The Takeaway: Choose Wisely, Not Just Excitedly

A niche can be the key to success – or a trap that sinks your business before it even starts. The best niches are ones that:

- Solve a real problem, not just a trendy one.
- Are big enough to sustain a business but narrow enough to dominate.

- Allow room for expansion and evolution.
- Have healthy margins – not just revenue, but actual profit.
- Are defensible, meaning big companies won't easily steamroll over them.

Juicero, Clubhouse and Limouzine all had interesting ideas, but they didn't check these boxes. That's why they faded.

Selecting a niche isn't just about finding an opening. It's about making sure that opening leads somewhere sustainable. Ultimately, success isn't about starting big. It's about starting *smart*.

- **Picking a niche is about choosing right, not choosing big** – the fit matters more than size.
- **Use the Three-Fit Test:**
  1. **Market Fit**: Is there real demand? Are people actively seeking a solution?
  2. **Founder Fit**: Do you have the passion, insight and edge to serve this niche well?
  3. **Defensibility**: Can you protect your position from copycats or larger players?
- **Validate before You Build**: Test interest through landing pages, pre-orders and real conversations. Don't rely only on the minimum viable product (MVPs).

- **Avoid these Common Traps**:
  - Falling for trends without substance.
  - Choosing niches too small or too narrow to grow.
  - Ignoring margins and profitability.
  - Competing with giants without a clear edge.
- The best niches are ones that solve urgent problems, have a committed founder, allow growth, generate profits and are hard to copy.
- The right niche is one where you can win, grow and endure – not just one that sounds exciting.

HOW

7

MORE THAN A PRODUCT

CRAFTING A NICHE THAT STICKS

In 1975, in a small town in Oregon, USA, a running shoe company made an unusual bet. Instead of designing shoes for all runners, they zoomed in on a single problem: traction on wet surfaces. Bill Bowerman, the company's co-founder, didn't have a high-tech lab or a massive R&D budget. What he had was curiosity and his wife's waffle iron. He poured rubber into the iron's mould, creating a sole that gripped the ground like nothing else out there. That small, almost accidental innovation birthed Nike's 'Waffle Trainer' and set the company on the path to global dominance. But here's the thing – Nike didn't start with a grand vision of being the biggest sports brand in the world. It started with a niche.

This is the power of niche product design. A great niche product isn't a smaller version of a mainstream one. It's built differently. It's positioned differently. It's valued differently. It doesn't try to please everyone. It solves one problem for one kind of customer, and does it better than anything else.

Niche Product Design

So, how do you design for a niche? It comes down to three core principles:

- Niche products solve specific problems.
- A strong niche value proposition makes the difference.
- Simplicity wins – focus on the core.

Let's break these down.

1. Niche Products Solve Specific Problems

In the 1990s, a college student in the UK watched his father shave and noticed something odd. His dad, an engineer, spent more time cleaning his razor than actually shaving. The blades clogged too easily. Replacements were expensive. The whole experience felt frustrating. That student, Will King, saw a problem others ignored. Instead of designing another razor with more blades, he launched King of Shaves, a brand built around a single insight: shaving should be smoother, cheaper and hassle-free. His breakthrough? A lubricating shaving oil that made even the cheapest razors glide effortlessly.

That's how niche products win. They don't fight for attention in an overcrowded market. They find a frustration that's been overlooked and fix it in a way no one else has.

Similarly, when Mamaearth was launched, big players like Johnson & Johnson and Himalaya already dominated baby care. But Mamaearth spotted a gap – parents who wanted completely safe products and full transparency about ingredients in their formulation. Instead of competing on price or distribution, Mamaearth built its brand around trust and purity. And that single focus helped it carve out a space in an industry ruled by giants. By 2024, Mamaearth's parent company, Honasa Consumer Ltd, reported a revenue of ₹1,920 crore.

If you're designing a niche product, ask yourself:

- What is the single biggest frustration my audience faces?
- How do mainstream products fail them?
- If my product didn't exist, what workaround would they use instead?

If you can answer these, you're already ahead.

2. A Strong Niche Value Proposition

A niche product can't afford to be vague. It can't rely on broad claims like 'better quality' or 'affordable prices'. It needs a sharp, undeniable reason to exist.

When boAt entered India's personal audio market, it wasn't competing with JBL, Sony or Sennheiser on sound quality. That would've been a losing battle.

Instead, the company focused on a specific idea: stylish, bass-heavy wireless earphones built for young urban Indians. Their marketing wasn't about technical specs. It was about music, lifestyle and identity. And that's why boAt didn't just sell headphones – it built a movement.

A strong niche value proposition does three things:

- It addresses a clear pain point. ('This is made just for you.')
- It differentiates from mainstream options. ('You won't find this elsewhere.')
- It creates an emotional connection. ('This brand gets you.')

Look at these examples:

- Lenskart isn't just about eyewear. It's about stylish, affordable glasses without the hassle of physical stores.
- Royal Enfield doesn't sell motorcycles. It sells heritage, adventure and a riding culture.
- Chumbak doesn't sell just souvenirs. It sells belonging and cultural pride.

The best niche products aren't just things people need. They're things people identify with.

When crafting your value proposition, ask:

- If I had five seconds to explain why my product matters, what would I say?
- Does my product create an emotional connection?
- Can my niche audience describe my product in one sentence?

If your answer is unclear, sharpen it. In a niche, clarity is everything.

3. Simplicity Wins – Focus on the Core

In the 1980s, a small Swiss running shoe company noticed something strange: elite marathoners were cutting holes in their shoes. Why? Because running shoes trap too much heat. Instead of ignoring the problem, they leaned into it, designing lightweight, breathable shoes with 'cloud-like' cushioning. That insight birthed On Running, one of the fastest-growing running brands in the world. And it happened because they solved one problem better than anyone else.

The mistake many businesses make? Overcomplicating their product. They assume that more features make it better. But the best niche products are designed with restraint – removing everything that doesn't matter.

When designing a niche product, ask:

- What is that one feature my customer will care about the most?
- If I removed half of my product's features, would it still solve the core problem?
- Does every element of my design reinforce my niche positioning?

Zerodha, India's largest stock brokerage, is a perfect example. Before it launched, trading platforms in India were cluttered, complicated and full of hidden fees. Instead of adding more features, Zerodha stripped everything down to a simple, zero-commission, user-friendly experience. That focus helped it dominate the market. Starting in 2014, Zerodha was the first Indian brokerage to reach 1 million accounts. They did it in 2019, flying past established players like ICICI, HDFC, Mirae Asset Sharekhan and Motilal Oswal.

Less is more. Especially in a niche.

Most businesses try to appeal to as many people as possible. Niche businesses thrive because they don't. They don't dilute their product trying to please everyone. They don't compete on price, but on expertise. They don't add unnecessary features – they focus on what matters most.

Nike started with a better sole. boAt focused on bass-heavy sound. Mamaearth doubled down on certified, ultra-safe baby care. They weren't the biggest in the industry. But they were the best at what they did. And in a niche, that's what matters most.

The MVP Mindset: Why Niche Businesses Must Start Small to Win Big

In 1994, a struggling entrepreneur named Jeff had an idea. He wanted to create an online store that sold books. But instead of spending years perfecting the website, signing deals with publishers or opening warehouses, he did something counterintuitive – he launched quickly, with the simplest possible version of his idea.

His website was basic, almost crude. When customers placed an order, Jeff didn't have the books in stock. He'd buy them from a distributor and ship them himself. The whole system was improvised. And yet, within months, Amazon was selling books faster than anyone had imagined.

This was what we now call a minimum viable product (MVP) – the simplest, most stripped-down version of a product that still solves a problem. Instead of guessing what people wanted, Jeff Bezos tested it. Instead of assuming how customers would behave, he watched them.

For mainstream businesses, MVPs are useful. But for niche businesses, they're critical. A niche product, by definition, serves a smaller, more specific audience. If you get it wrong – if the problem isn't real, if the solution isn't compelling – you won't have millions of customers to fall back on. A niche business has to validate its idea early, before time, money and effort are wasted.

The MVP: What It Is and What It Isn't

In its purest form, an MVP is not a half-finished product – it's a fully functional product that tests your core idea. It's not about launching something incomplete. It's about launching something simple, but right.

Take Uber, for example. Before raising funds and becoming the world's favourite ride-hailing app, it started as UberCab, a basic service connecting riders with drivers via iPhones or SMS in San Francisco and New York. A human dispatcher coordinated the cabs.

Or take Facebook. Mark Zuckerberg initially launched Facemash, where users compared pictures, and then he created TheFacebook, a social network for Harvard, Stanford, Columbia and Yale students only. The lesson? You don't need a perfect product. You need proof that people want it.

Before launching retail stores or an expansive eyewear catalogue, Lenskart tested its idea with a home try-on programme – sending people frames for free and allowing them to try before they bought. This MVP allowed them to gauge customer interest and refine their sales model before investing in large-scale production.

Why MVPs Matter Even More in a Niche Market

If you're launching a product for a mass market, you have room for error. You can afford some missteps, knowing that a limited percentage of the population will still buy what you're offering.

But in a niche, the stakes are higher. You're targeting a smaller, more specific audience, which means:

- If you get it wrong, there's no backup plan. You can't just pivot to another customer base – the whole point of a niche is that it's tightly defined.

- You need to test assumptions early. Mainstream businesses can afford expensive market research. Niche businesses need real-world feedback as fast as possible.
- Speed matters. If a niche exists but remains unserved for too long, someone else will fill the gap.

A niche product, by definition, solves a highly specific pain point. The MVP allows you to test if the pain point is real enough, urgent enough and profitable enough to build a business around.

When boAt entered India's personal audio market, it didn't launch a full line of speakers, headphones and earbuds. It started with one product: an affordable, stylish, bass-heavy wireless earphone for young, urban Indians.

Instead of over-engineering its offering, boAt focused on what mattered most to its target audience:

- **Affordability**: It was priced lower than premium brands like JBL and Sony.
- **Style**: The products were designed to look premium despite the budget pricing.
- **Bass-Heavy Sound**: It was perfectly tailored for India's Bollywood and EDM-loving audience.

The result? boAt became the #1 personal audio brand in India – not because it had the most advanced technology, but because it nailed the niche before it began expanding.

In the 2000s, trading in India meant paperwork, expensive broking, unreliable trading processes, etc. But instead of launching with every trading feature imaginable, Zerodha focused on one thing: zero-commission trading with a simple interface.

By stripping away complexity, it attracted first-time investors who would have otherwise been intimidated by stock markets. It started with an MVP that worked, and expanded only after proving demand.

Each of these companies validated their niche before scaling – ensuring they didn't waste time building something no one wanted.

Building the Right MVP for Your Niche

Creating an MVP entails carving out the simplest version of your idea that actually solves the core problem, delivers real value to users and gives you quick feedback to learn what to build next.

1. Identify the Core Hypothesis

Before building anything, ask yourself:

- What assumption am I making about my niche? (Example: 'Young professionals in Mumbai will pay extra for an organic meal delivery service.')
- What's the fastest way to test if that assumption is correct?

For Licious, the fresh meat delivery brand, the assumption was, 'People will pay a premium for high-quality, hygienic meat.' Their MVP? Selling fresh-cut meat from a single facility and delivering in small batches before scaling up.

2. Start with the Simplest Functional Version

The goal of an MVP is not to impress. It's to learn.

- If you're launching a subscription box, don't wait until you have a perfect logistics setup. Offer a one-time curated box first and measure demand.
- If you're launching a personalized skincare brand, don't develop twenty products at once. Start with one – a single formulation for a specific problem.
- If you're starting a local food delivery business, don't build an app from scratch. Test the demand for it by taking WhatsApp orders first.

3. Get Feedback and Iterate

An MVP is useless if you don't learn from it. Your first launch won't be perfect – but that's the point.

- What do customers love? Double down on it.
- What do they ignore? Cut it out.
- What confuses them? Simplify.

Amazon started with books. Now it sells everything.

boAt started with wireless earphones. Now its portfolio includes everything from smartwatches to soundbars.

Zerodha started with zero-commission trading. Now it offers wealth management and investment tools.

But none of them started big. They started right.

A niche business doesn't have millions of customers to experiment with. It has a specific audience with specific needs – and if those needs aren't understood early, the whole business can fail. If you're building for a niche, don't aim for perfection. Aim for proof. Because in a niche, the worst mistake isn't launching small. It's launching big and wrong.

The Importance of Being Important: Why Niche Businesses Must Matter Deeply

In 2014, a tiny start-up in Mumbai was struggling to gain traction. They were selling cold-pressed juices, a concept that was popular in the West but largely unheard of in India. Their bottles were beautifully designed, the branding was slick and the product was genuinely high quality. But sales were sluggish. The few customers they had liked the juice, but no one seemed to need it.

Then, something unexpected happened. A handful of Mumbai's elite fitness trainers started recommending the brand to their celebrity clients. Suddenly, the same juice that had been ignored was being treated like a necessity – something that wasn't just nice to have, but essential to a certain lifestyle.

That brand was Raw Pressery, and within a year, it had exploded. The lesson? It wasn't enough to be *good*. It had to be important to someone.

The Invisible Versus the Indispensable

Every business exists on a spectrum: at one end, you have products that are easily replaceable, and at the other, products that are deeply necessary.

A generic ballpoint pen? Replaceable.

Your morning cup of coffee? Necessary.

A high-end wristwatch? Replaceable.

The insulin that a diabetic needs every day? Necessary.

The difference? How deeply the product matters to the customer's life.

The problem many niche businesses face isn't competition – it's indifference. They make something good, they market it well, but then fail to become important. And in a niche market, if you're not important, you're irrelevant.

Who Would Miss You If You Disappeared?

A veteran from the early days of Dropbox, LogMeIn and Eventbrite, Sean Ellis, had a puzzle to solve. These were good products – clever, well-designed, genuinely useful – but the usual indicators of success weren't telling him much. Revenue? Too slow to develop. User growth? A vanity metric. Market share? A lagging indicator at best. By the time you knew whether a company was a hit or a flop, it was already too late.

Ellis needed a leading indicator, something that would predict success before it happened. And so, he devised a deceptively simple question: *How would you feel if you could no longer use this product?*

Users had three choices:

- Very disappointed.
- Somewhat disappointed.
- Not disappointed.

Then, Ellis started testing. He ran this survey across nearly a hundred start-ups, looking for patterns. And a pattern emerged. Companies that struggled to gain traction almost always had fewer than 40 per cent of users saying they'd be 'very disappointed' without the product. Companies that took off? They almost always exceeded that 40 per cent mark. It was an inflexion point, a signal that a product had crossed from 'nice to have' into 'can't live without'.

Consider Slack. When Ellis's test was run on Slack's user base, 51 per cent of respondents said they would be very disappointed without it. That's an extraordinary number. Slack didn't just have users – it had devotees. People didn't just like the product; they depended on it. This explains why Slack isn't just another communication tool. It's a workplace staple.

Now, compare that to Superhuman. By all conventional wisdom, Superhuman should not exist. It's an email app with a $30-a-month price tag, in a world where Gmail is free. And yet, Superhuman doesn't just exist – it thrives, with its ultra-fast, keyboard-driven productivity. But it didn't start that way. When Superhuman first ran Ellis's test, only 22 per cent of users said they'd be very disappointed without it. By Ellis's benchmark, that was a failure.

Most companies would have seen that number and panicked. Superhuman's founder, Rahul Vohra, did something else. He drilled down. Instead of trying to make Superhuman appeal to everyone, he asked a different question: *who are the people that would be very disappointed without it?*

The answer? Super-busy professionals – founders, executives, investors. People who lived in their inboxes and craved speed. Instead of watering down the product to win over the masses, Superhuman doubled down on this core audience. It refined its focus. It got sharper, not broader: adding AI-assisted drafting, natural-language search, split inboxes, read receipts and team collaboration.

And something remarkable happened. The 22 per cent grew. By relentlessly improving for the right people, Superhuman inched closer to the 40 per cent threshold.

The Three Paths to Importance

Imagine your business suddenly vanished tomorrow. Would your customers simply switch to something else? Or would they feel like they lost something they truly needed? The most successful niche businesses are the ones that embed themselves so deeply into their customers' identity or routine that they become irreplaceable.

Take Dyson. Before Dyson, vacuum cleaners were just another household appliance. But Dyson redefined the category – not just with better suction, but by turning vacuuming into a high-tech experience. Today, Dyson's customers don't just own a vacuum cleaner. They own a Dyson.

Or think about CrossFit. It's not just a gym. It's a movement. People who do CrossFit don't just exercise – they identify as CrossFitters. They wear the brand, speak the language and build their social lives around it. It's not just fitness; it's a lifestyle.

These brands aren't just selling something. They are part of their customers' sense of self. That's the kind of importance that niche businesses need to aim for.

There are three primary ways a niche business can become important to its customers:

1. Solve a Deep, Emotional Pain Point

Not all problems are felt problems. Some are mild inconveniences. Others hurt. The deeper the pain point, the more important your solution becomes.

- YourDOST became important because people are deeply burdened by unspoken stress and need a safe space for mental wellbeing.
- Nutrizoe became important because new mothers are deeply anxious about postpartum nutrition and need trusted, supportive solutions for recovery.

- PeeSafe became important because women are deeply concerned about hygiene and safety in public spaces, especially while traveling.

Customers don't buy products. They buy relief from a problem that bothers them enough to take action.

2. Become Part of Their Identity

A niche business thrives when it isn't just selling something – it's helping customers say something about themselves.

- Apple isn't just a tech company. It's a statement about design, innovation and individuality.
- Royal Enfield isn't just a bike. It's about a rugged, adventurous spirit.
- Fabindia isn't just a clothing brand. It's a bridge between tradition and modernity, a way to wear cultural pride.

The more a product aligns with a customer's sense of self, the harder it is to replace.

3. Integrate into Their Daily Routine

The most successful businesses don't just serve a need. They become part of a habit.

Think of:

- The first app you open in the morning (WhatsApp, Instagram, Gmail).

- The drink you reach for in the afternoon (Red Bull, Nescafé, Paper Boat).
- The ritual you never skip (morning skincare, a daily workout, checking your investments).

A niche business that integrates into daily life becomes impossible to ignore.

Don't Just Exist. Matter

Too many businesses focus on being an alternative instead of being the one. For example, most organic food brands market themselves as 'healthier' alternatives to mainstream brands. But what if they positioned themselves as the only option for true food purists? Similarly, most D2C skincare brands talk about 'gentle formulas'. But what if they became the brand dermatologists personally recommend for sensitive skin? Instead of trying to compete broadly, become the favourite of a specific group, not just another option.

The biggest risk in business isn't failure. It's being forgettable. A niche business doesn't need millions of customers. It needs a small group of people who can't imagine life without it. Because in the end, success doesn't come from being available. It comes from being important.

- **Niche products aren't just smaller versions of mainstream.** They are deeply focused, purpose-built solutions to specific problems.
- **Three core principles of niche product success:**
  1. **Solve a Specific Pain Point**: Like Mamaearth or King of Shaves, success comes from fixing one real frustration better than anyone else.
  2. **Craft a Sharp Value Proposition**: Clear, bold messaging that resonates emotionally (e.g. boAt, Paper Boat).
  3. **Keep It Simple**: Focus on the core feature or benefit; strip away the noise (e.g. Zerodha, On Running).
- **Start with an MVP**: Build the simplest version that tests your core idea, like Amazon, Lenskart or Superhuman. Don't wait for perfection, and validate early.
- **Niche Businesses must Matter Deeply**: To succeed, a product must feel indispensable to its users – not just useful.
- **Three ways to become important**:
  1. Solve a deep, emotional pain point.
  2. Become part of the customer's identity.
  3. Integrate your product or service into their daily routine.
- The best niche products don't just exist – they matter. They win by being the most important thing for a few, not everything to everyone.

8

BUILT FOR THE FEW, LOVED BY MANY

NICHE PRODUCT STRATEGIES

In 2007, a small brand called Oatly was struggling to break through. The Swedish company had developed an oat-based milk alternative, but supermarkets weren't interested. Almond milk and soy milk dominated the shelves, and oat milk felt like an afterthought. So instead of chasing the mass market, Oatly made a bold decision: it would focus on a single niche – baristas.

Cafés had a problem. Most plant-based milks didn't foam properly, making it difficult to create the silky micro-foam needed for lattes and cappuccinos. Oatly's research team tweaked their formula, creating a milk alternative that steamed just like dairy. Then, they went door to door, convincing independent coffee shops to try it.

The bet worked. Baristas loved it. Coffee enthusiasts took notice. Oatly became a cult favourite, and by the time it hit supermarket shelves, it wasn't just another plant milk – it was *the* oat milk that cafés used. Today, Oatly is a billion-dollar brand, but it did not start with the masses. It started with a niche that needed it most.

This is the paradox of niche products. They are built for the few, but when done right, they resonate far beyond their intended audience. Tesla didn't start with affordable electric cars – it started with a high-performance sports car for enthusiasts. Crocs were originally designed for boaters, but they became a fashion statement. The best niche products don't just serve a small market – they create loyalty so intense that their influence spreads.

This chapter is about understanding that process. There are six product strategies for niche businesses introduced here, and many times, niche businesses may use more than one at a time.

1. Bespoke and Mass Customization
2. Scarcity- and Exclusivity-Driven Positioning
3. Luxury and Premiumization
4. Craftsmanship- and Heritage-Driven Branding
5. Performance- and Utility-Driven Specialization
6. Ethical and Sustainability-Driven Positioning

1. Bespoke and Mass Customization: The Art of Making It Just for You

In an era of mass production and algorithmic recommendations, there's something profoundly special about knowing that a product was made just for you. Not just selected from a menu of pre-existing options, but crafted, designed and tailored to your exact needs, preferences and quirks. This is the promise of bespoke products – a world where every detail is shaped around the individual. It's not just about exclusivity; it's about personal relevance. And in the world of niche businesses, this is one of the most powerful ways to build deep, lasting customer loyalty.

Luxury has always been synonymous with customization. Think of a Savile Row suit, where master tailors meticulously measure, cut and stitch every inch of fabric to match the wearer's posture, proportions and style. It's not just about clothing; it's about identity. The same logic applies to bespoke jewellery, handcrafted leather shoes and personalized fragrances. But today, the idea of tailoring products to individual preferences is no longer limited to the ultra-wealthy. Advances in technology and manufacturing have made mass customization possible, allowing brands to offer uniquely personal products at scale.

Consider SkinKraft, India's first AI-driven personalized skincare brand. Instead of customers picking a generic product off the shelf, SkinKraft asks them to take a detailed skin assessment. The company then formulates a routine specifically for their skin type – dry, oily, combination, acne-prone, sensitive – factoring in everything from climate conditions to lifestyle choices.

It's not just another skincare brand; it's a relationship, one that feels like having a dermatologist in your pocket.

Personalization has also disrupted footwear. Nike By You, formerly NikeID, allows customers to tweak everything from material and colour to the laces and sole pattern of their shoes. The underlying product remains the same, but by giving people control over the final look, Nike transforms a commodity into something deeply personal. In India, Lego-like modular shoe brands have begun to emerge, offering urban customers the ability to swap out parts of their sneakers based on mood, function or even weather conditions.

Then there's the world of automobiles. Royal Enfield, the legendary Indian motorcycle brand, has introduced customization options that allow riders to modify their bikes straight from the factory. Everything from the handlebars to the seat finish to the colour scheme can be adjusted, giving customers a sense of ownership that goes far beyond a standard showroom purchase. Enthusiasts don't just ride a Royal Enfield – they design their own.

Where bespoke and mass customization differ is in their approach to scale. Bespoke is deeply personal, time-intensive and high-touch – designed for those who value craftsmanship and exclusivity above all else. It requires a deep understanding of customer preferences, often demanding a more consultative sales approach. It can be harder to scale, as customization inherently adds complexity to manufacturing and fulfilment.

Mass customization, on the other hand, is about offering personal touches within a controlled framework. It operates within predefined limits – modular selections, preset templates or AI-driven recommendations – but still allows customers to feel like they're part of the creation process. It delivers uniqueness at scale, making it a powerful tool for niche businesses that want to differentiate without becoming operationally unmanageable.

Both models share a common advantage: they create a far stronger emotional connection between customer and brand. When a product is made specifically for you – even within a defined structure – it stops being just another purchase. It becomes a statement, a reflection of who you are. And this, in turn, makes customers far less price-sensitive. If a mass-market item is too expensive, a customer might look for a cheaper alternative. But if something is crafted to their exact needs, switching costs become high – not just financially, but psychologically. That's why businesses built on hyper-personalization tend to enjoy higher margins and stronger customer retention.

Yet, when executed well, bespoke and mass customization create more than just revenue; they create relationships. They move beyond transactions and into the realm of trust, where customers see the brand not as a business, but as a partner in their self-expression. In a world increasingly dominated by mass production and automated recommendations, the brands that make people feel truly seen will always have a place.

Because at the end of the day, what's more niche than something made just for you?

2. Scarcity- and Exclusivity-Driven Positioning: The Business of Making People Want What They Can't Have

It's a curious thing about human nature – we always seem to want what we can't have. The more difficult something is to get, the more desirable it becomes. If a product is rare, hard to find or available only to a select few, it stops being just another option and transforms into something far more powerful: a status symbol, a marker of taste, a badge of belonging. Scarcity isn't just a pricing strategy; it's a psychological trigger, one that makes people crave something even before they fully understand why.

This is the foundation of scarcity-driven businesses. They operate not by maximizing availability, but by deliberately restricting it. Some limit production, some limit access and others create artificial constraints around time and availability. The result? Customers chase the brand rather than the brand chasing customers.

Take Supreme, the American streetwear phenomenon,

making waves globally. Every Thursday, Supreme 'drops' a limited batch of clothing, accessories and skateboards. These items are never restocked. Once they're gone, they're gone forever. The result? People line up for hours – sometimes days – outside Supreme stores. Resellers flip items at two, three, even ten times the retail price. The company doesn't need to advertise; the fans do that for them. The entire business thrives on the simple idea that if everyone can have something, no one wants it.

In India, Manyavar applies a similar scarcity-driven approach, though with a cultural twist. Weddings are the ultimate status event in Indian society, and Manyavar has positioned itself as the go-to choice for grooms, groomsmen and wedding guests. Their designs follow a seasonal cycle, ensuring that styles are refreshed constantly. If you miss out on a particular sherwani or bandhgala, you won't find it the next year. Manyavar doesn't sell everyday clothing; it sells exclusivity for life's biggest moments.

Then there's Rolex, the ultimate example of engineered scarcity. Rolex produces only a limited number of watches each year, despite their overwhelming demand. Walk into a Rolex store today, and you'll find most models marked 'Out of Stock'. Authorized dealers maintain waiting lists that stretch into years. This isn't a supply chain issue; it's a deliberate strategy. Rolex doesn't want its watches to be easy to buy. The act of acquiring one is part of the brand's mystique.

Scarcity doesn't always have to mean low volume. Sometimes, it's about access. Amex's Centurion Card, better known as the Black Card, isn't something you can apply for. You have to be invited. There are no advertisements, no billboards, no celebrity endorsements. The secrecy fuels the allure, turning it into one of the most coveted credit cards in the world. In India, something similar exists with exclusive whisky clubs, where certain limited-edition bottles are available only to select members.

But while scarcity can create demand, it's a delicate game. Done wrong, it can alienate customers and limit growth. Done right, it can elevate a niche brand into a cultural icon. The trick is in balancing availability with desirability – releasing just enough to build demand, but never so much that the brand loses its aura of exclusivity.

Scarcity works best when it feels natural. If a company limits supply purely as a gimmick, customers see through it. But when scarcity is built into the DNA of the product – whether through craftsmanship, seasonality or insider access – it becomes a self-sustaining engine of demand. People don't just want the product; they want to be part of the world it represents.

Ultimately, what's more desirable than something you can't have?

3. Luxury and Premiumization

Somewhere in Mumbai, a man walks into a car showroom, but he's not there to buy a car. He's already on the waitlist for a Mercedes-Maybach, and his purchase is all but guaranteed. Instead, he's there to choose the stitching on his seats, the shade of his wood trim and whether the logo on the headrest should be embroidered in platinum or gold. His car, when it arrives, will be a masterpiece of customization, a statement of status, and most importantly, an object of exclusivity.

At the other end of the city, a woman steps into a Forest Essentials store. She could have bought a moisturizer for ₹200 at the pharmacy down the street, but instead, she's holding a jar of night cream infused with saffron and 24K gold and worth ₹3,500. The packaging is exquisite, the branding whispers heritage and indulgence and the store experience feels more like a high-end spa than a retail outlet. She isn't just buying skincare; she's buying a ritual, a feeling, a piece of luxury.

This is premiumization – the process of taking an everyday product and elevating it into something aspirational, something people are willing to pay significantly more for. It's not just about raising prices; it's about fundamentally altering the perception of value.

The Three Pillars of Premiumization

Luxury isn't just about expense. It's built on three

pillars: perception, experience, and scarcity.

1. Perception: The Story Is the Product

A Rolex doesn't just tell time, and a Sabyasachi lehenga isn't just fabric and thread. What people are really buying is the story – the craftsmanship, the exclusivity, the aura of something rare and meaningful. Luxury brands don't just sell products; they sell narratives.

When Veeba started as a niche B2B supplier of sauces and condiments for fast-food chains, it wasn't a premium brand. But when it entered the consumer market, it completely rebranded itself as a gourmet experience. The packaging looked artisanal, the flavours were international and the messaging was all about quality over quantity. It wasn't ketchup – it was 'chipotle mayo', and suddenly, it was worth paying extra for.

2. Experience: The More You Charge, The Better It Must Feel

Walk into a Louis Vuitton store anywhere in the world, and the experience is the same: plush interiors, personal attention and an air of exclusivity. You don't 'shop' at Louis Vuitton; you're guided through a carefully curated journey.

The same playbook works for niche brands. Nicobar, a contemporary Indian fashion and lifestyle brand, sells clothing, homeware and travel accessories – but what it really sells is a lifestyle. Its stores are designed like boutique homes, its website feels like a high-end fashion magazine and its branding suggests that by owning Nicobar, you are part of an elite, well-travelled, design-conscious tribe.

The premium isn't just in the product; it's in the way you buy it. The checkout process, the packaging, the post-purchase experience – all of it must feel superior. That's why luxury hotels give you handwritten notes, why Apple products come in satisfying, slow-opening boxes and why Tesla owners don't deal with pushy salespersons but get direct delivery from the company itself.

3. Scarcity: Luxury is a Club, Not a Market

True luxury is not mass-produced. It is deliberately constrained. MB&F watches, for example, are not just expensive because they're finely made – they're expensive because they're rare. Each model has a limited run, and once it's sold out, it's gone. The exclusivity makes it more desirable.

But scarcity isn't only about production limits. It can also be about distribution. Nappa Dori, the premium Indian leather goods brand, doesn't sell everywhere. You won't find it in mass-market department stores. It maintains exclusivity through limited outlets, carefully selected retail partnerships and a brand image that suggests owning a Nappa Dori piece is an insider's choice.

The takeaway? If you want your niche brand to be premium, don't be available everywhere. Control where and how people access your product.

How to Apply Premiumization to Any Niche Business

- **Craft a Strong Narrative**: Why does your product deserve to be premium? Is it made differently? Sourced uniquely? Does it tie into a cultural or historical tradition?
- **Control the Experience**: From packaging to purchase, the way customers interact with your brand should feel elevated.
- **Create Scarcity**: Limit availability, either through production numbers, distribution channels or time-bound editions.
- **Price Confidently**: Premium brands don't justify their prices. They set the price and let the perception do the rest.

Luxury and premiumization are not just about high prices. They're about making people want to pay more. And when done right, people don't just buy your product. They buy into your world.

4. Craftsmanship- and Heritage-Driven Branding

At a small workshop in Jaipur, a *karigar* (artisan) leans over a block of wood, carefully carving out an intricate floral pattern. His hands move with precision, muscle memory passed down through generations. In another part of the country, deep in Kutch, women sit together embroidering fabric, their stitches so fine that a single square inch can take hours to complete. These crafts are not just skills; they are the inheritance of centuries.

But for a long time, no one was buying.

Traditional Indian craftsmanship was struggling. Fast fashion was cheaper, mass production was more scalable and consumers, even in India, were shifting toward synthetic fabrics and factory-made goods. Then, something changed. Artisans didn't just need customers – they needed a brand that told their story in a way modern buyers could appreciate.

Luxury brands have always known the power of craftsmanship. A Hermès Birkin bag is crafted by a single artisan and takes up to forty-eight hours to make, entirely hand-stitched. A Patek Philippe watch is assembled by master horologists who train for a decade before they're allowed to work on the brand's most intricate timepieces. The message is simple: the longer it takes, the better it must be.

Indian niche brands are now using the same playbook. Raw Mango, the handwoven textile brand founded by Sanjay Garg, didn't just sell saris – it sold a revival of India's rich weaving traditions. The brand positioned itself as more than just a clothing label; it was a cultural statement. When you buy a Raw Mango sari, you're not just paying for the fabric. You're paying for history, for craftsmanship, for something that couldn't have been made by a machine.

Similarly, Brass Tacks, a Chennai-based fashion label, took khadi – often seen as a symbol of political nostalgia – and made it chic. By modernizing silhouettes while retaining traditional handloom techniques, it transformed khadi from a fabric of the past into a luxury material for the present.

One of the biggest advantages niche brands have is that they can tell a deeper, more personal story than mass-market brands ever can. The beauty of heritage-driven branding is that it creates an emotional connection with the buyer. It's the difference between owning a generic wool scarf and owning a Pashmina shawl that has been handwoven in Kashmir using centuries-old techniques.

Nappa Dori reintroduced traditional Indian leather craftsmanship in a contemporary way. The products have a distinct vintage-meets-modern aesthetic, and their handcrafted nature gives them a uniqueness that mass-produced leather brands can't replicate.

In the food space, Paul & Mike is a great example. This Indian bean-to-bar chocolate brand uses cocoa grown in Kerala and emphasizes ethical, small-batch production. While multinational chocolate brands flood the market with industrially processed bars, Paul & Mike uses fermentation techniques and handcrafting methods to create chocolates that rival the world's best artisanal brands.

How to Build a Craftsmanship-Driven Niche Brand

1. **Make the Process Part of the Story**: If your product is handcrafted, show it. Whether through videos, packaging or brand messaging, let customers see the effort and skill that goes into what they're buying.
2. **Elevate the Artisans**: Many niche brands succeed by making their makers the stars. Showcasing the people behind the product – whether it's weavers, metalworkers, leather artisans or perfumers – adds depth and authenticity.
3. **Modernize, but Don't Dilute**: The key to success isn't just preserving traditional techniques; it's adapting them for contemporary tastes. Whether it's textiles, jewellery or even home decor, craftsmanship should feel timeless, not outdated.
4. **Price for Perception**: Craftsmanship carries value, and the pricing should reflect that. A handmade product should never try to compete with mass-market goods on price – it should compete on experience, authenticity and exclusivity.

In a world where everything is becoming automated and digital, craftsmanship offers something irreplaceable: human touch. That's why a hand-stitched mojari from Rajasthan feels different from a factory-made leather shoe, and a hand-painted blue pottery vase from Jaipur holds more charm than its machine-made counterpart.

For niche brands in India, the opportunity is clear. Craftsmanship and heritage aren't relics of the past. They are powerful branding tools – ones that can turn a niche product into an icon, a community into a movement and a business into a legacy.

5. Performance- and Utility-Driven Specialization: Built to Perform

In 2016, a small engineering company in Coimbatore designed a tool that only a handful of people in the world needed. It was a precision-cutting machine for aerospace components, built to specifications so demanding that no off-the-shelf solution existed. Their clients weren't regular businesses; they supplied to the Indian Space Research Organisation (ISRO) and Hindustan Aeronautics Limited (HAL) – organizations that couldn't afford failure. Every micron mattered. Every cut had to be perfect.

This is the essence of utility-driven specialization. The best niche businesses don't just serve a market; they solve a problem in a way that no one else can. Some do this with technology, others with superior craftsmanship and some by understanding the user's needs better than anyone else.

When Function Comes First

Many of India's most successful niche brands have

been built not on luxury, exclusivity or heritage, but on performance. They identify a gap in functionality – something missing in mainstream alternatives – and build something so good that customers have no reason to look elsewhere.

Take Sleepyhead, a D2C mattress brand that figured out a fundamental flaw in the Indian market: traditional mattresses were bulky, difficult to transport and confusing to buy. They solved this with a simple but revolutionary idea – a mattress-in-a-box. The mattress was compressed, rolled and shipped in a compact package that customers could unbox and set up themselves. It eliminated the need for middlemen, made logistics easier and provided a better product than what was available in showrooms.

A similar story played out in the world of backpacks. Harissons Bags, a legacy brand from Mumbai, understood that young professionals and students needed backpacks that could keep up with their changing lifestyles. Their bags weren't just designed for carrying things; they had anti-theft compartments, USB charging ports and ergonomic back support – features that transformed them from a simple storage solution into an essential everyday tool.

The 'Best-in-Class' Advantage

In many cases, a niche product doesn't need to appeal to everyone – just to those who demand the best. This is why FootJoy dominates the golf shoe market, Hasselblad cameras remain the gold standard for professional fashion photographers and Steiner binoculars are trusted by the military. They don't aim for mass adoption. They aim for performance so exceptional that their niche customers never consider anything else.

This is exactly how Candes built its niche in India's home appliance market. Competing with giants like Bajaj and Crompton in the ceiling fan business seemed impossible – until Candes focused on durability and energy efficiency as its key differentiators. They built fans with stronger motors, longer warranties and lower power consumption, targeting buyers who wanted a better fan, not just a cheaper one. Today, they dominate their niche without ever having to compete on price.

Performance: How to Get it Right

Not all niche businesses can rely on storytelling or luxury pricing. Some have to prove themselves through sheer performance. Here's how businesses in this space make their mark:

- **Solve a Real Problem, Not Just a Perceived One**: The best utility-driven niche brands don't just claim to be better; they prove it. The key is to find an inefficiency – something that frustrates customers – and design a solution so good that switching becomes a no-brainer.
- **Be Obsessive about Quality**: When a product's

value is tied to performance, there's no room for mediocrity. Brands like Stanley (which makes unbreakable thermos flasks) and Bosch (which builds precision power tools) thrive because their customers trust them not to fail.

- **Charge for Value, Not Cost**: A niche product that performs better than its mainstream counterparts shouldn't compete on price. Whether it's a high-end kitchen knife, an ergonomic office chair or a premium water purifier, customers will pay more for something that demonstrably works better.
- **Earn Your Reputation through Results**: A great niche product doesn't need aggressive marketing. When performance is the differentiator, customers become evangelists. In India, this is how Agrim Wholesale, a B2B e-commerce start-up for agricultural tools, grew – farmers who found their products more reliable spread the word faster than any advertising campaign could.

Why Utility Always Wins

At the heart of it, performance- and utility-driven niche businesses succeed because they give customers what they actually need. They don't sell a dream. They solve a problem. Whether it's a highly functional backpack, a hyper-efficient home appliance or an industrial-grade precision tool, these businesses prove that when a product is designed to perform better, it creates its own market.

For Indian entrepreneurs looking to carve out a niche, this approach holds massive potential. In a market as diverse and fast-growing as India, there will always be an unfulfilled need, an inefficiency waiting to be solved, a way to make something functionally better. Those who find it – and build the best possible solution – will own their space, no matter how big or small.

6. Ethical and Sustainability-Driven Niche Brands: Doing Well by Doing Good

In 2013, a young engineer named Vinu Daniel stood at a construction site in Kerala, staring at a mountain of waste. He wasn't looking at discarded food or plastic – he was looking at construction debris, tons of broken bricks and concrete chunks that were destined for a landfill. Most builders saw this as unavoidable. Vinu saw it as raw material.

He started experimenting, using waste as a core ingredient in building construction. Over time, his firm, Wallmakers, developed a method to construct entire buildings using compressed earth blocks, salvaged debris and sustainable materials. Today, his projects – beautiful, functional and eco-friendly – stand as proof that sustainability isn't just an ethical choice. It can be a niche business strategy.

Niche businesses thrive by serving a specific, often underserved, audience. And increasingly, one of the most powerful differentiators is a commitment to sustainability, ethics and social responsibility. Customers today, especially in India's urban and millennial segments, aren't just looking for what a product does. They care about how it's made, who makes it and what impact it has on the planet.

Look at Bare Necessities, a Bengaluru-based start-up that sells zero-waste personal care and home products. In a market flooded with chemical-laden shampoos and single-use plastic packaging, they built their brand around an ethical promise: no plastic, no harmful chemicals, no waste. Their customers aren't just buying a product – they're buying into a philosophy.

This is the power of sustainability-driven positioning. It's not about slapping a green label on a product; it's about baking ethics into the core of the business model. And when done right, it turns a niche into a movement.

The Scarcity of Trust

The rise of ethical brands isn't just a feel-good trend; it's a response to a crisis of trust. Over the past decade, Indian consumers have grown wary of mass-market brands. Food scandals, environmental damage and unethical labour practices have made customers sceptical.

This is why brands like No Nasties, one of India's first 100 per cent organic and fair-trade clothing labels, have found their niche. The brand, founded in Goa, built its entire value proposition around traceability – every cotton T-shirt and dress is made from ethically sourced cotton, manufactured with fair wages and sold with full transparency. Customers don't just buy the clothes; they buy peace of mind.

This strategy works because trust is a rare commodity, and the brands that earn it can command both customer loyalty and premium pricing.

The Business Case for Ethics

Many entrepreneurs assume that ethical and sustainability-driven businesses appeal only to a niche audience – urban elites willing to pay more for a feel-good purchase. But the reality is much broader.

Consider Jaipur Rugs, a company that revolutionized the traditional carpet industry by eliminating middlemen and empowering rural artisans. Instead of treating weavers as cheap labour, Jaipur Rugs positioned them as skilled creators, giving them fair wages, access to global markets and recognition for their craftsmanship. The result? A business that sells handwoven rugs across the world at premium prices – proving that ethical business is good business.

Ishka Farms pioneered sustainable organic caper farming in Tamil Nadu. Caper farming wasn't an industry in India; it was something most people associated with Mediterranean cuisine. But Ishka saw an opportunity – not just to build a farm, but to do so using organic, regenerative agriculture. Today, their capers are sold globally, and the farm is a model for sustainable, high-value agriculture.

For an entrepreneur looking to build a niche business with an ethical or sustainability-driven edge, the key is authenticity. Customers today can sense greenwashing from a mile away. The businesses that succeed aren't the ones that talk about being sustainable – they are the ones that live it.

That means embedding sustainability into the product itself. For a brand like Paper Crush, which sells eco-friendly stationery, the product isn't just paper – it's a statement against deforestation. For Okhai, a social enterprise selling handcrafted apparel, the clothes aren't just fabric – they are stories of empowerment for rural women.

The most successful ethical brands also focus on transparency. They tell the customer exactly where the product comes from, who makes it and why it matters. This level of openness builds trust and loyalty – something most mass-market brands can't replicate.

As consumers in India become more conscious of the environmental and social impact of their choices, ethical and sustainability-driven businesses will no longer be just a niche – they will become a necessity. The entrepreneurs who understand this shift early, who embed ethics into their business model rather than treat it as an afterthought, will be the ones who thrive.

Ultimately, niche businesses succeed when they offer

something unique, valuable and meaningful. And there are few things more meaningful than building a business that does well by doing good.

- **Niche products often start by solving a very specific problem for a small audience**, but if done right, they gain passionate loyalty that fuels broader appeal (e.g., Oatly, Tesla, Crocs).
- **Niche product strategies fall into six key types**:
  1. **Bespoke and Mass Customization**: Personalised products build loyalty and perceived value (e.g., SkinKraft, Royal Enfield).
  2. **Scarcity and Exclusivity**: Deliberate limitation drives demand and creates desirability (e.g., Supreme, Rolex).
  3. **Luxury and Premiumization**: Turn everyday products into aspirational experiences by focusing on perception, experience and scarcity (e.g., Forest Essentials, Nicobar).
  4. **Craftsmanship and Heritage**: Revive traditional skills to offer authenticity and emotional connection (e.g., Raw Mango, Nappa Dori).
  5. **Performance and Utility**: Solve problems better than anyone else with a focus on function and quality (e.g., Candes, Sleepyhead).

6. **Ethical and Sustainable**: Build trust through transparent and responsible practices (e.g., Bare Necessities, No Nasties, Jaipur Rugs).

- Each strategy appeals to a different type of customer and need, but they all rely on the same core insight: build something that matters deeply to someone, and it will matter to many.
- Great niche products win because they are intensely relevant, not widely average. They create emotional connections, solve real problems or reflect values – and that's what makes them spread.

9

THE STORY YOU SELL

BRANDING, PRICING AND PERCEPTION

In 2010, a little-known luggage company in Mumbai started with a simple but radical idea: why were Indian travellers stuck choosing between overpriced international brands and cheap, flimsy suitcases that barely survived a single trip? There was no in-between – no brand that was stylish, durable and designed for the unique needs of Indian travellers.

So, they built one. Nasher Miles didn't try to compete with Samsonite or VIP on price or size. Instead, it positioned itself as the luggage brand for modern Indian travellers – sleek, lightweight and packed with features that mattered (like 360-degree wheels for uneven Indian airport surfaces). Instead of targeting 'everyone who needs a suitcase', it spoke directly to urban, experience-driven travellers. Today, Nasher Miles is one of the fastest-growing travel brands in India – not because it sells luggage, but because it sells an identity. A Nasher

Miles cabin luggage may cost upwards of ₹5,000, whereas some of the large brands have offerings below ₹2,000 as well.

This is the essence of brand-building in niche businesses. A great niche brand doesn't just sell products. It creates a world, a personality, a point of view – one so specific that it becomes irreplaceable to the people who connect with it.

Mainstream brands succeed by being safe, broad and familiar. They don't want to alienate anyone. They speak in generalities, appeal to the middle of taste and price and ensure their messaging resonates with millions of people.

Niche brands don't have that luxury. They have to own an idea completely, even if that means ignoring 90 per cent of the market. The key to successful brand-building in a niche business is:

- Specificity over mass appeal. If everyone likes your brand a little, no one will love it passionately.
- Personality over neutrality. People should be able to describe your brand like a person: bold, quirky, elegant, rebellious.
- A clear point of view. A niche brand should feel like it believes in something – so strongly that it attracts *some* and repels *others*.

Blue Tokai understood this instinctively when it set out to redefine India's relationship with coffee. Before it arrived, coffee was either instant (Nescafé, Bru) or expensive café culture (Starbucks, Café Coffee Day). There was no real Indian specialty coffee brand. So Blue Tokai gave itself a personality – the thoughtful coffee connoisseur, someone who cares deeply about craft, origin and flavour. It didn't just talk about 'premium coffee'; it talked about Indian farmers, single-estate beans and freshly roasted perfection. The visual language was minimalist and earthy, evoking small-batch craftsmanship rather than big-chain efficiency. Everything about the brand suggested that drinking Blue Tokai wasn't just about getting caffeine – it was about participating in a movement.

That kind of specificity is what makes a brand unforgettable.

Owning a Story

The strongest brands have stories that customers can explain in one sentence. Tesla makes electric cars cool. Amul is 'the taste of India'. Chumbak is quirky Indian design in everyday life. The best niche brands build narratives that spread.

Paper Boat didn't invent fruit juice. But it did something smarter – it made childhood nostalgia its brand story. Its drinks weren't just about taste; they were about memories: summer afternoons with grandparents, train journeys with a flask of home-made aam panna.

The packaging was handwritten, personal, almost like a letter. The brand voice felt like an old friend reminiscing about simpler times. By making itself about emotion rather than just function, Paper Boat created a brand that people *felt* – not just consumed.

Creating Rituals, Not Just Products

Great brands don't just sell things. They create experiences. They become part of people's daily lives, habits and personal identities. Apple doesn't just sell iPhones – it sells the ritual of unboxing. Starbucks isn't just coffee – it's a break, a moment, a lifestyle. Manyavar isn't just clothing – it's the uniform for Indian celebrations.

Phool isn't just incense – it's devotion transformed into sustainability, a way to pray without polluting rivers. Emoha isn't just eldercare – it's companionship and dignity for seniors, and peace of mind for their children.

Forest Essentials understood this when it positioned itself as more than just a skincare brand. It became a ritual – an indulgent return to India's Ayurvedic roots. The elegant gold-and-cream packaging felt regal. The fragrances and textures were designed to feel immersive. The entire experience of using the product felt less like applying lotion and more like partaking in an ancient self-care tradition. That transformation – from commodity to ritual – is what turns customers into loyalists.

The Power of Visual Language

A niche brand should be instantly recognizable, even without its name. The colour, font, photography style and logo should all feel like part of a cohesive world. Fabindia never needed flashy ads. Its stores, branding and colours felt like India itself – earthy, rooted, deeply authentic. The deep indigo and beige tones evoked natural fabrics. The minimalist store layouts kept the focus on the craft. Even the hand-drawn fonts reinforced the feeling of something handmade. Without saying a word, Fabindia's visual language told its story.

Consistency Is Everything

The most successful niche brands don't chase trends. They repeat their message until they become synonymous with their niche. Nykaa stayed laser-focused on beauty until it became India's beauty authority. Bira 91 stayed quirky and young until it became India's first true craft beer. boAt focused on stylish, affordable audio until it became the lifestyle-tech brand of choice.

Repetition isn't boring – it's how brands become memorable.

Niche brands don't win by trying to be big. They win by being unforgettable to the right people. In a world overflowing with choices, people don't remember products. They remember brands that make them feel something.

The Price of Being Special: A Niche Business Guide to Pricing

In 2012, a tiny chocolate brand in Bengaluru made a bold move. It launched a single bar of chocolate for ₹350 – a price that seemed absurd in a country where you could buy a Dairy Milk for ₹10. There were no celebrity endorsements, no flashy advertisements, just an elegant wrapper with a simple promise: handcrafted, bean-to-bar chocolate, made in India, using only the finest cacao.

That brand, Soklet, became India's first tree-to-bar chocolate maker and, in the process, redefined the way Indians thought about chocolate. It wasn't just a sweet treat anymore – it was an indulgence, a luxury, something to be savoured, not mindlessly eaten. The high price wasn't a deterrent; it was a signal. It told customers that this wasn't chocolate for the masses – it was chocolate for those who appreciated the craft behind the product.

Soklet is about rooted authenticity, chocolate that wears its Indian terroir on its sleeve, celebrating origin, purity and tradition. Paul & Mike, similar but different, are about global ambition, taking Indian cacao to the world stage with bold innovations, experimental flavours and a modern, playful identity.

For niche businesses, pricing is not just about cost and profit margins. It's about storytelling. A price tag communicates whether a product is exclusive or accessible, premium or mass-market, worth waiting for or easy to ignore. The right price creates perceived value, filters out the wrong customers and builds brand credibility.

But pricing a niche product is also a delicate balancing act. Set it too low, and customers assume it's inferior. Set it too high, and they might walk away. Unlike mass-market brands, niche businesses don't have the luxury of making up for pricing mistakes with sheer volume. Every transaction matters. Every customer matters. So, getting the price right is everything.

Pricing 101: Basics Every Niche Business Needs to Know

Before diving into strategy, it's important to understand the fundamental pricing models available:

- **Cost-Plus Pricing**: The simplest approach, it means calculating production costs and adding a markup. This works well in industries where margins are thin, but for niche products, this method often undervalues the emotional and experiential aspects of pricing.
- **Value-Based Pricing**: This approach prices the product based on what customers are willing to pay, rather than just production costs. A ₹100 incense stick from Nirmalaya isn't about the cost of raw materials – it's about the idea of sustainable, hand-rolled, pure and clean luxury.

- **Competitive Pricing**: This involves looking at similar products in the market and pricing accordingly. It works in mass markets but is less relevant for niche businesses, where you are often creating a category rather than entering an existing one. If Tesla had priced itself against Maruti Suzuki, it would have never redefined electric cars.

For most niche businesses, a combination of value-based pricing and strong brand-driven perception is the sweet spot.

The Power of Premium Pricing in Niche Businesses

Customers don't just evaluate price – they evaluate context, experience and meaning. A ₹300 coffee seems expensive – until it's served in a Japanese ceramic cup at a Third Wave Coffee café, where everything, from the lighting to the brewing method, whispers craftsmanship. The price doesn't just buy coffee; it buys a feeling, an identity, a moment.

Premium pricing works for niche businesses because:

- It reinforces exclusivity. Higher prices filter out casual buyers, attracting those who truly value the product.
- It shapes brand perception. People assume that a product priced higher is better made, more exclusive and of superior quality.

- It builds loyalty. Customers who pay a premium feel more invested in the brand and become its best advocates.

Sabyasachi never tried to be 'affordable fashion'. It positioned itself as couture for Indian weddings – painstakingly crafted garments steeped in heritage, showcased with opulent campaigns, and priced to signal exclusivity. The high price made it aspirational. It wasn't for everyone – but that was precisely the point.

For niche businesses, premium pricing isn't just about charging more. It's about creating an experience that justifies the price.

When Price Becomes a Weakness: The Danger of Discounts

Mass-market brands rely on discounts to drive volume. Amazon runs sales every other week. Myntra survives on 'flat 50% off' banners. But in niche businesses, discounts can be dangerous.

A premium tea brand that suddenly offers 40 per cent off risks losing its credibility. A ₹3,000 silk scarf that drops to ₹1,200 in a sale makes customers wonder if it was ever worth ₹3,000 in the first place.

That doesn't mean niche businesses should never discount. It just means discounts should be used strategically. Here are three smart, selective discounting strategies:

- **First-Time Customer Offers**: A small, one-time discount can encourage trial without devaluing the brand. For example, Sleepy Owl Coffee offers a ₹100 discount on the first order, but never runs mass sales.
- **Loyalty-Based Discounts**: Instead of cutting prices for everyone, reward existing customers with perks. Nicobar doesn't do site-wide discounts, but it offers early access to collections and exclusive events for its most loyal shoppers.
- **Limited-Time Pricing Moments**: Instead of random sales, niche brands can create special pricing events: 'Festival Edition', 'Founders' Anniversary Offers' or 'Limited Batch Releases'. Paul & Mike regularly introduce special edition craft chocolate bars that are available for just a few months, keeping demand high without devaluing regular products.

The key is to maintain pricing integrity. Once a niche brand starts discounting too often, customers stop seeing it as premium – and that's a hard reputation to rebuild.

What Happens When Pricing Goes Wrong

A price tag can elevate a brand – or kill it. When Tata launched the Nano, the world's cheapest car, it should have been a success. But it wasn't. Why? Because no one wanted to drive 'the cheapest car'. The pricing was so aggressive that it worked against the product. People didn't see it as affordable – they saw it as something they'd be embarrassed to own.

At the other end, when OYO Rooms tried to launch a premium hotel segment, it struggled. Customers associated OYO with budget stays, and they weren't willing to pay higher prices for a brand that was already positioned as cheap. If pricing doesn't match brand perception, it creates confusion, and confusion kills brands.

This is why niche businesses need to get pricing right from the beginning. If you want to be premium, be premium. If you want to be accessible, own that positioning. But never try to be both. For niche businesses, pricing isn't just about making money. It's about what the brand stands for, who it speaks to and how customers perceive it.

The best niche businesses don't compete on price. They compete on meaning.

The Price of Meaning: Value-Based Pricing for Niche Products

In 2017, a small engineering firm in Pune did something radical. Instead of competing on price like every other industrial supplier, it flipped the script. It started charging more than its competitors for custom machine components used in pharmaceutical factories.

At first, this seemed absurd. The industry was cut-throat, and procurement managers were trained to squeeze suppliers on cost. But this company, Adinath International, had a different strategy. It wasn't just selling machine parts – it was selling reliability, precision and compliance with international quality standards. The message was clear: if a ₹20-lakh machine in a pharmaceutical plant failed because of a substandard ₹5,000 part, the real cost wasn't ₹5,000 – it was millions in lost production, regulatory fines and damaged reputation. The fact that Adinath was not just a machine parts supplier but one that specialized in the pharmaceutical industry also helped a lot.

Customers started seeing value, not just price. Soon, the same procurement managers who had scoffed at their rates were now willing to pay the premium.

This is the essence of value-based pricing – charging not based on what something *costs to make*, but based on the value it delivers to the customer.

For niche businesses, value-based pricing is often the only sustainable model. Whether you're in B2B (industrial equipment, software as a service [SaaS], speciality consulting), B2C (luxury, organic, handcrafted) or D2C (premium personal care, artisanal foods, specialized fitness gear), success comes from owning a problem, solving it better than anyone else and pricing accordingly.

Most traditional businesses use cost-plus pricing – they take the cost of raw materials, labour and overhead, add a percentage markup and set the price. This works when selling commodities, but niche products aren't commodities.

A handcrafted Kanjeevaram sari isn't priced based on silk and zari costs. It's priced based on:

- **Heritage**: The 150-year-old weaving tradition behind it.
- **Craftsmanship**: The skill of artisans who take months to weave a single piece.
- **Exclusivity**: The idea that each sari is unique, never mass-produced.

Similarly, a boutique cybersecurity firm doesn't price its services based on the number of hours spent writing code. It prices based on the cost of a data breach – which could be millions for a client.

The biggest failure of cost-plus pricing is that it ignores customer perception of value.

Value-Based Pricing in B2B: The Hidden Profits in Specialization

B2B buyers don't care about features – they care about outcomes. The more clearly a product or service translates into higher revenue, lower risk or faster operations, the higher its perceived value.

Take ideaForge, an Indian drone company. It doesn't sell drones based on the cost of manufacturing. It sells 'unmanned aerial intelligence' for defence, infrastructure and mining companies. If an ideaForge drone helps the Indian Army detect threats more accurately, its value isn't ₹10 lakh per unit – it's lives saved, missions secured and operational efficiency.

Or consider Altigreen, a start-up that builds commercial EVs for urban logistics. If a fleet operator switches from diesel vans to Altigreen's EVs and saves ₹1.5 lakh per year on fuel and maintenance, then Altigreen isn't selling a vehicle – it's selling annual cost savings. That's how you justify premium pricing in B2B – by linking price to business impact. How niche B2B businesses use value-based pricing:

- **Price Relative to Cost Savings**: If a product cuts costs by ₹10 lakh per year, charging ₹2 lakh is an easy sell.
- **Price Relative to Risk Avoidance**: A ₹25-lakh insurance software isn't expensive if it prevents a possible ₹100 crore in fraud.
- **Price Relative to Revenue Growth**: If AI-powered sales software boosts revenue by 20 per cent, charging 5 per cent of the increase is reasonable.

The secret? Make the customer see the cost of *not* buying.

Value-Based Pricing in B2C and D2C: The Price of Identity and Emotion

In consumer markets, value isn't just about performance – it's about identity, experience and meaning.

A Jade Forest tonic water isn't just sparkling water with botanicals – it's the perfect pairing with a premium gin. A Tanjore painting isn't just wall decor – it's a piece of heritage. A No Nasties organic cotton T-shirt isn't just soft fabric – it's ethical fashion that tells a story about who you are.

Consumers don't calculate value the way B2B buyers do. Their perception of worth is shaped by psychology, branding and storytelling.

How niche B2C businesses use value-based pricing:

- **Scarcity = Higher Perceived Value**: If a brand makes only 500 bottles of a single-batch gin, people want it more.
- **Lifestyle Positioning**: A ₹12,000 pair of handcrafted leather shoes from The Shoe Factory is about elegance, not just durability.
- **Emotional Benefit**: Parents buy Slurrp Farm organic baby food not for taste, but for peace of mind.

In D2C, smart brands justify price with purpose. They educate customers about why they charge more – through storytelling, behind-the-scenes content and transparency about sourcing and labour. This is why Sabyasachi can sell a ₹4,00,000 lehenga – because it positions itself not as clothing, but as couture: painstakingly handcrafted, rooted in heritage and designed to be heirlooms. The price isn't just about fabric or embroidery, it's about exclusivity and aspiration.

When Pricing Too Low Is Worse Than Pricing Too High

There's a common fear in niche businesses: 'If I charge too much, no one will buy.'

But the opposite is often true. Under-pricing creates doubt. It makes customers ask:

- Why is this so cheap? Is something wrong with it?
- If it's really premium, why isn't it priced like it?
- Will this brand survive if they're charging so little?

Luxury brands understand this well. No one asks why a Rolex costs ₹8 lakh – they assume it's worth it. But if a 'luxury' watch was priced at ₹8,000, people would immediately doubt its authenticity.

For niche businesses, higher pricing often drives higher trust. If you've positioned your product correctly, the right customers will pay – because price reinforces credibility. Pricing isn't math. It's a narrative. A niche brand doesn't just sell a product – it sells an outcome, a feeling, a solution to a very specific problem. The best niche businesses don't price based on cost. They price based on what the customer gains by choosing them. Value isn't what a product *is* – it's what a customer *feels* about it.

- **Niche brands succeed by being specific, not broad**. They sell identity, emotion and belief, not just products (e.g., Nasher Miles, Blue Tokai).
- **Great niche brands have:**
  - A strong personality and point of view.
  - A compelling origin or story that spreads (e.g., Paper Boat, Forest Essentials).
  - Visual consistency that builds recognition (e.g., Fabindia).
- **Pricing is part of branding**. It signals value, aspiration and intent. Premium pricing can build credibility, loyalty and trust.
- **Niche businesses thrive with value-based pricing**. Charging based on what the product means to the customer, not just what it costs to make.
- **Discounts can damage brand perception**. Use them sparingly and strategically to reward loyalty or drive limited-time excitement.
- **In B2B and D2C alike**, premium prices are justified when you clearly solve high-value problems or deliver identity and emotional resonance.
- **In a niche, your story is your strength**. Both your brand and your price should reflect what your product *means* to your customers – not just what it does.

10

FINDING YOUR PATH

THE CHANNELS THAT MAKE NICHES WORK

In 2016, a young entrepreneur couple in Delhi had a problem. They had spent months perfecting a chemical-free, paraben-free skincare product for babies, but no big retailer was willing to take it seriously. The shelves at supermarkets were controlled by legacy brands like Johnson & Johnson and Himalaya, and the purchasing managers at big-box stores had a simple response: *'Indian parents don't care about "natural" skincare. If they did, the big brands would already be doing it.'*

So, they decided to do something radical. Instead of trying to beg their way into retail, they launched online and, through their website, went straight to their customers. They didn't need the approval of retailers – they needed the trust of parents.

That brand was Mamaearth, and today it's a ₹10,000-crore company. Mamaearth didn't become a

D2C success story because it had the best baby products. It won because it broke free from the traditional retail playbook. It didn't fight for shelf space – it built its own. It didn't wait for customers to *discover* it – it went directly to them. For niche brands, D2C isn't just a channel. It's a mindset shift. It allows brands to:

- Own their brand story, without middlemen filtering the message.
- Control pricing, margins and customer relationships.
- Experiment, iterate and refine the experience based on direct customer data.

The big brands still rely on large distributors, traditional advertising and mass retail networks. But the most successful niche businesses? They own their sales channels, starting with their website.

Why a Website Is the Core of a Niche D2C Brand

Many niche brands make the mistake of thinking that listing on Amazon, Flipkart or Nykaa is enough. After all, these platforms have massive traffic, right?

Sure. But here's the problem.

In 2019, Makaibari, an artisanal tea brand from Darjeeling launched on Amazon. They had handpicked single-origin teas, packaged beautifully, with detailed tasting notes. But when a customer searched for 'Darjeeling tea', their ₹799 premium tin appeared right next to a ₹250 pack from Tata Tea.

Guess what happened? The cheaper tea got almost all of the sales.

Marketplaces prioritize price and convenience over storytelling and brand differentiation. If your brand doesn't stand out visually and emotionally, you're just another stock-keeping unit (SKU) in an endless catalogue.

A niche brand's website isn't just an online store. It's the digital flagship, the equivalent of having your luxury boutique on Fifth Avenue – except it's open 24/7, and you don't have to worry about rent. Consider The Whole Truth, a niche clean-label D2C brand that took on the Indian protein snack industry. Instead of listing their bars on Amazon and disappearing into a sea of competitors, they made their website the primary shopping destination.

- They controlled the messaging. No confusing product descriptions, just bold, clear storytelling.
- They controlled the experience; right from unboxing to email follow-ups, everything felt curated.
- They collected first-party data, understanding exactly what customers liked and tailoring offers accordingly.

Compare this to selling on Amazon or Flipkart, where:

- Your product sits next to thousands of competitors, often with price being the only differentiator.

- The customer relationship belongs to the marketplace, not you – you don't even get their email.
- Discounts and pricing wars force you into thin margins and constant battles for visibility.

Owning your website means owning the customer experience. That's why successful niche D2C brands use marketplaces strategically – as an acquisition channel, not the main business.

- Use Amazon/Flipkart for discovery, and direct customers to your website for repeat purchases.
- Differentiate website pricing. Offer special bundles, exclusives or first-time discounts.
- Retarget marketplace buyers with email and social media to bring them into your ecosystem.

This is how brands like Man Matters (men's wellness), Flatheads (premium sneakers) and Bare Anatomy (customized hair care) operate – they exist on marketplaces, but they thrive on their own websites.

A niche D2C website isn't just an online store – it's a brand experience. The best ones have:

- **A Strong Narrative**: Customers should immediately understand the brand's mission (e.g., 'The cleanest protein bars in India' for The Whole Truth).
- **A Seamless Checkout**: If it takes more than two to three steps, customers drop off.

- **Clear Pricing Transparency**: No hidden costs, no surprises.
- **First-time Purchase Incentives**: Discounts, free shipping or a bonus item encourage conversion.
- **Subscription or Bundle Options**: Encouraging repeat purchases increases lifetime value.

For example, Country Bean Coffee's website makes it effortless to subscribe to their flavoured coffee blends. Instead of a one-time purchase, they nudge customers toward monthly deliveries, ensuring long-term loyalty.

Owning Pricing and Margins: The Biggest D2C Advantage

One of the most overlooked benefits of D2C is pricing control.

In traditional retail, margins are brutal. By the time a product reaches the shelf, retailers take 30–50 per cent, distributors take another 10–20 per cent and marketing spends keep adding up. For a ₹1,000 product, the brand might only get ₹350–₹400.

D2C eliminates these middlemen. If a brand sells directly, it can keep 70–80 per cent of the price. This is why niche businesses can afford to charge premium rates – they are not subsidizing a massive distribution network.

This is part of the reason why boAt sells premium audio gear at a fraction of JBL's price, Sleepy Owl keeps its cold brew affordable despite using premium beans and SkinKraft personalizes skincare without retail markups. By controlling their own pricing, niche D2C brands can offer better products at the same price – or premium products at justified premiums.

In traditional retail, launching a new product is slow, expensive and risky. A company has to negotiate with retailers to even get shelf space and spend months on packaging and positioning before launch. Even then, they have to invest heavily in mass marketing to get noticed.

D2C brands? They move fast.

When Anveshan, an artisanal food brand, wanted to test a new cold-pressed mustard oil, they didn't wait for supermarket approvals. They launched it on their website with a limited batch of 1,000 bottles. If it worked, they'd scale. If it didn't, they'd tweak the formula and try again.

This kind of agility is impossible in traditional retail. D2C allows brands to experiment, get real-time feedback and optimize products before making big commitments.

Niche brands don't succeed by being everywhere. They succeed by owning their audience, their brand and their growth.

The Art of Being Found: How Niche Brands Win on Social Media

In 2019, an independent sneaker brand in India did something bold. They didn't launch with a massive marketing budget. They didn't flood Instagram with ads. They didn't partner with Bollywood celebrities.

Instead, they put out a single post – a close-up shot of a sleek, minimalist sneaker with the caption: *'Designed for Indian feet. Built for Indian streets.'*

That one post, from a then-unknown brand called Flatheads, caught fire. Comments poured in – people wanted to know more. What made them different? Were they better than Nike? Did they actually feel different on Indian roads? The intrigue built up, and within a few weeks, their first batch of sneakers sold out completely – without spending a single rupee on traditional advertising.

This is what social media does for niche brands.

Unlike mass-market giants that push their way into consumer consciousness with big ad budgets, niche businesses have to earn their place. They can't afford to buy attention – they have to attract it. And social media, when used right, is their secret weapon.

If a mass-market brand like Pepsi posts on Instagram, it's just another reminder of something you already know. It's background noise – a billboard in digital form. But if a hyper-specific brand – say, a handcrafted ukulele maker from Goa – posts on social media, it's different. It's a discovery. It's unexpected. It's an invitation into a subculture. For niche businesses, social media isn't about trying to be everywhere. It's about being deeply relevant somewhere.

The most successful niche brands use social media to:

- Tell a compelling story. Not just what they sell, but why they exist.
- Find the right audience. People who genuinely care, not just casual scrollers.
- Spark engagement, not just awareness. Because niche brands need loyalty, not just visibility.

But to do this well, they need to stop thinking like advertisers and start thinking like community members.

The Right Platform for the Right Niche

Not all social media platforms work for every niche. A brand selling luxury artisanal perfumes doesn't need to be on Twitter. A B2B SaaS tool doesn't need a thriving Instagram page. The secret to winning on social media is to choose the right battleground.

1. Instagram: The Home of Aesthetic Storytelling

For brands that are visual, experiential and aspirational, Instagram is non-negotiable.

Take Nicobar, that sells clothing, home decor and accessories with a modern Indian aesthetic. Their

Instagram isn't just a product showcase – it's an entire world. A Nicobar post doesn't just say 'Buy our kurta' – it evokes a feeling of slow, conscious living, of lazy Sunday mornings and handwritten letters.

Instagram works for niche brands that sell:

- Fashion, beauty and lifestyle (e.g., The Pant Project, Fabindia).
- Artisanal and handmade goods (e.g., Karu, Bare Necessities).
- Wellness and personal care (e.g., Kama Ayurveda, Juicy Chemistry).

It's not just about *posting*. It's about:

- **Aesthetic Consistency**: Making the feed feel like an experience.
- **Interactive Content**: Polls, Q&A, reels that spark engagement.
- **User-Generated Content (UGC)**: Getting customers to share their moments with the brand.

If done right, Instagram doesn't just drive sales – it makes people aspire to be part of the brand's world.

2. Twitter: The Voice of Thought Leadership

If Instagram is for aesthetics, Twitter is for ideas.

B2B and knowledge-driven brands thrive here – not because they post ads, but because they own conversations.

Consider AngelList India, which helps start-ups raise capital. They don't use Twitter to sell. They use it to share insights on investing, start-up trends and funding stories. This makes them an authority, and authority builds trust.

Twitter works for niche brands that sell:

- B2B products and services (e.g., SaaS tools, fintech solutions).
- Tech, start-ups and innovation-driven products.
- Educational and knowledge-based businesses.

Winning here isn't about selling. It's about:

- Providing value via insightful threads, case studies and industry trends.
- Engaging in real conversations by responding to trending topics in your niche.
- Being consistent with building a reputation, tweet by tweet.

For a niche business that wants credibility and trust, Twitter can be more powerful than any ad campaign.

3. YouTube: Long-Form Trust Building

If a niche brand needs depth, trust and education, YouTube is unbeatable.

The Blue Tokai Coffee Roasters YouTube channel isn't just about selling coffee – it's about coffee culture. They post videos on how to brew the perfect cup, how different roasts affect flavour and why freshly ground beans matter.

This does two things:

- It positions them as experts. Customers don't just buy coffee from them; they *learn* from them.
- It builds brand trust. People who watch their videos are far more likely to buy from them.

YouTube works for brands that need:

- Education-based marketing (e.g., skincare science, sustainable living).
- Step-by-step tutorials (e.g., cooking, fitness, DIY crafts).
- In-depth storytelling (e.g., brand origin stories, behind-the-scenes content).

If done well, YouTube doesn't just create customers – it creates fans.

4. LinkedIn: The B2B Powerhouse

For niche businesses in enterprise, SaaS, consulting or high-ticket B2B sales, LinkedIn is the place to be.

Companies like Freshworks (India's first SaaS unicorn) built massive brand awareness by using LinkedIn to share:

- Customer success stories discussing real-world case studies of businesses they helped.
- Posts that offer industry insights and free knowledge before selling anything.

- Personal branding of the founders to make the brand feel human and accessible.

If your niche business targets decision-makers, founders and professionals, LinkedIn isn't optional – it's critical.

Most brands fail at social media because they treat it like a billboard – something to display their products and hope people notice.

But the best niche brands treat social media like a conversation. They:

- **Listen First**: They understand their audience's problems before trying to sell.
- **Engage Meaningfully**: They don't just post; they interact, reply and add value.
- **Create Shareable Moments**: Making their brand something people *want* to talk about.

Even as social media opens doors for niche brands, it comes with risks that cannot be ignored. Algorithms are opaque and ever-changing; what works today might vanish from visibility tomorrow, throttled by an update no one saw coming. Ownership is another grey area. Your content, your followers and even your brand voice can be subject to platform policies and intellectual property disputes. And in some countries, entire platforms have been banned overnight due to regulatory or political reasons, wiping out years of digital equity. For brands that build entirely on borrowed platforms, the ground beneath is far from stable. The smart ones treat social media as an amplifier, not the foundation, always anchoring their brand presence in spaces they fully control, like their own website and community.

For a niche business, social media isn't about reaching the most people. It's about reaching the right people, in the right way, with the right message. The brands that win aren't the ones that shout the loudest. They're the ones that make people stop scrolling and pay attention.

The Right People Talking: How Niche Brands Build a Band of Influencers

If you wanted to buy a car twenty years ago, you'd go to a dealership. A well-dressed salesperson would greet you with a practised smile, hand you a glossy brochure and deliver a perfectly rehearsed pitch about fuel efficiency, safety features and financing options.

Fast forward to today, and the first thing most people do before buying a car is open YouTube. They'll watch a real person – not a corporate ad – break down every detail, from the way the car handles in city traffic to whether the back seat is comfortable for a long drive.

The same thing is happening everywhere. Whether it's a ₹2-lakh DSLR camera, a ₹5,000 sari or a ₹500 face serum, people don't trust brands. They trust people. This is why influencer marketing has become the new word-of-mouth – and why, for niche brands, it isn't just an option. It's a necessity.

But here's where most brands go wrong.

They think influencer marketing is about paying celebrities to talk about their product. It's not. Real influence isn't about followers. It's about trust. The best niche brands don't buy influence – they build it. They find the right voices, the right platforms and the right ways to tell their story; so that when people hear about them, it feels authentic, not scripted.

Types of Influencers That Actually Work for Niche Brands

If you're selling Colgate toothpaste or Samsung phones, you can throw money at Bollywood actors, Instagram stars and cricketers, and millions of people will see your product. But if you're selling a handcrafted, vegan leather laptop bag made by artisans in Pondicherry, a mass-market influencer is useless. Their audience is too broad. The message will get lost.

Niche brands don't need mass exposure. They need the right exposure. That's why the best niche brands work with influencers who are trusted within specific communities.

- A luxury Ayurveda skincare brand like Forest Essentials doesn't need a Bollywood star – it needs a skincare expert who understands Indian herbs and rituals.

- A specialty coffee brand like Blue Tokai doesn't need a generic food influencer – it needs a barista or coffee reviewer who actually knows the difference between single-origin and blend.
- A performance running shoe brand like Saysh doesn't need a fashion model – it needs a runner who can break down how the shoes perform on the racetrack.

The lesson? The smaller and more focused the influencer, the stronger the impact.

The biggest mistake niche brands make is chasing big numbers. A travel influencer with 3 million followers might get you views, but a hiking enthusiast with 30,000 followers might actually get you sales. For niche brands, the best influencers fall into these categories:

1. Subject Matter Experts (SMEs) – Trusted for Knowledge

SMEs are the people who actually know what they're talking about. They are scientists, fitness trainers, chefs, musicians or industry professionals who have built credibility because of their expertise, not their follower count. For example, Rachna Chhachhi, with a PhD in nutrition, reviews healthy food brands and is trusted more than generic food influencers. Similarly, Gaurav Chaudhary (Technical Guruji) is far more influential in the gadget world than a Bollywood actor promoting a smartphone. This is because they have deep credibility. If they say something is good, people believe them.

2. Community Leaders and Niche Celebrities – Trusted for Subculture Influence

These are people who aren't famous to the mainstream but are iconic in their specific world. A yoga instructor with 15,000 devoted students is more valuable for a yoga mat brand than a general fitness influencer with 1 million followers. A top stand-up comedian reviewing a premium laptop is more influential for creative professionals than a generic lifestyle blogger. Similarly, a craft beer brewer talking about a new local microbrewery will drive more real engagement than a food blogger covering hundred restaurants.

Why do they work? They are deeply connected to their audience – they don't just have followers, they have fans.

3. Passionate Micro-Influencers – Trusted for Authenticity

A few years ago, Savana decided to get into the fast fashion business. This was getting to be a crowded space, with Indian companies like Trent and Zudio, and multinationals like Zara, H&M, Mango and others. They decided to build their brand with the help of micro-influencers.

The result was something money couldn't easily buy: authenticity. Instead of polished, scripted endorsements, these micro-influencers shared honest reviews. Their followers – many of whom were also exploring plant-based or sustainable lifestyles – listened, engaged and, most importantly, cared. A small but passionate community began to form, bound not by advertising but by genuine belief in the product.

This is the power of micro-influencers, with followings between 5,000 and 50,000. They work for three key reasons. First, their engagement rates are higher. With fewer fake followers and more real conversations, their recommendations feel organic. Second, they feel personal. Unlike celebrities who broadcast content to millions, micro-influencers reply to comments, interact and build relationships. And third, they're cost-effective. While big-name influencers charge staggering fees, often running into lakhs, micro-influencers are far more accessible – sometimes promoting products in exchange for free samples or modest payments.

For niche brands, this strategy isn't just an alternative; it's a competitive advantage. One hundred passionate micro-influencers can drive more meaningful impact than a single big-name influencer ever could. Because in the world of niche marketing, influence isn't about numbers – it's about trust.

The Right Way to Work with Influencers

Most brands approach influencer marketing with a predictable formula. Find a famous person. Pay them to pose with your product. Hope for a spike in sales. It's a straightforward playbook, but for niche brands, it rarely works.

The best brands take a different approach – one that values authenticity over reach and relationships over transactions. First, they make it about the influencer, not themselves. No one wants to sound like a walking advertisement, least of all influencers who have built their reputation on trust. The smartest brands give them the freedom to tell their story in a way that feels natural, weaving the product into their narrative rather than forcing a scripted promotion.

Second, they think long-term. A single, one-off post feels like an ad. But an influencer who repeatedly engages with a brand? That feels like a genuine endorsement. The most effective partnerships aren't transactions; they're relationships. That's why successful brands collaborate with the same influencers over time, building credibility with each interaction.

And third, they offer an experience, not just a product. Sending a pair of running shoes to a sneaker reviewer is fine. Sending them to a trail running event where they can put the shoes to the test? That's something memorable. When influencers experience a product in a way that aligns with their audience's lifestyle, their endorsement doesn't feel like marketing – it feels like a story worth sharing.

Selling Without Selling: How Niche Brands Win with Affiliate Marketing

In 2018, Disguise Cosmetics, a small home-grown vegan skincare brand in India faced a problem. They had no budget for big ads, no celebrity endorsements and no way to compete with the deep-pocketed giants like Mamaearth and Plum that dominated Instagram and Amazon. Instead of trying to outspend the competition, they did something different.

They partnered with a network of small, passionate influencers, bloggers and niche community leaders – people who already talked about clean beauty, sustainability and cruelty-free skincare. Instead of paying them up front, they gave them a commission on every sale they drove. Within two years, this tiny brand had scaled into a multi-crore business, fuelled almost entirely by word-of-mouth and affiliate marketing.

For niche businesses, affiliate marketing isn't just about driving sales – it's about building an army of advocates. It's a way to get other people to sell for you, without upfront risk, while keeping your brand authentic. But done wrong? It turns into a spammy, discount-driven mess.

Done right? It can build an entire ecosystem of trust and recommendation-driven sales.

What Affiliate Marketing Really Is (and What It Isn't)

Affiliate marketing has a reputation problem. Many people associate it with sketchy coupon websites and clickbait bloggers looking to make a quick commission. But at its core, affiliate marketing is just word-of-mouth – amplified by incentives.

Unlike traditional influencer marketing, where brands pay upfront for a post, affiliates earn only when they drive real results. It's a simple but powerful shift. Niche bloggers, who might otherwise talk about brands for free, now have a reason to consistently share and recommend products they truly believe in. Brands, instead of sinking money into uncertain ad campaigns, pay only for actual conversions.

For niche brands, this changes everything. Instead of pouring money into visibility, they can focus on rewarding the people who are already passionate about their product. It's not just marketing – it's a way to turn real advocates into growth engines.

Why Affiliate Marketing Is a Perfect Fit for Niche Businesses

If you're selling a mass-market shampoo, affiliate marketing might not be your best strategy. Big-brand products succeed because of name recognition, wide retail availability and competitive pricing. Consumers grab them off the shelf without much thought.

But if you're selling a handcrafted, all-natural Ayurvedic hair oil made in small batches, the decision to buy isn't impulsive – it's intentional. Customers want to know the ingredients, the benefits and, most importantly, whether they can trust the brand. And that's where affiliate marketing excels.

It works because it's built on trust. Consumers are far more likely to listen to an independent recommendation than believe a direct advertisement. If a well-known beauty influencer with curly hair swears by an oil that tames frizz, that endorsement carries far more weight than a generic ad ever could.

It's also hyper-targeted. Instead of spending money on broad, untargeted ads, brands pay only for real conversions – customers who are genuinely interested and ready to buy. Every affiliate isn't just a marketer; they're an advocate, helping spread awareness without brands needing to push aggressively.

And perhaps the most powerful advantage? It's risk-free scaling. Unlike traditional influencer marketing, where brands pay upfront and hope for results, affiliate marketing flips the model. Payment happens only when a sale goes through.

The best affiliate programmes don't feel like marketing. They feel like recommendations from people you already trust. Here are some brands that have used such trust-based networks to scale smartly:

- **The Whole Truth (Clean Food and Snacks)**

The Whole Truth used a referral and affiliate system to grow. Instead of splurging on influencer promotions, they built a programme where fitness coaches, dieticians and micro-influencers earned commissions by recommending their bars and spreads.

- **Kapiva (Ayurvedic Nutrition and Wellness)**

Kapiva, a modern Ayurveda brand, partnered with yoga teachers and holistic health influencers to promote its herbal supplements and drinks. Since Ayurveda needs education and credibility, they used trusted voices to sell the benefits, not just the product.

- **Sleepy Owl (Specialty Coffee)**

Coffee brands thrive on loyalty and ritual. Sleepy Owl built an affiliate structure where coffee bloggers, home brewers and even small café owners could earn commissions by driving subscriptions and first-time buyers.

- **Zymrat (Performance Wear)**

Zymrat, a high-performance men's sportswear brand, partnered with running coaches, gym trainers and CrossFit influencers – people who had credibility in the fitness space – to drive traffic directly to their website instead of relying on marketplaces like Amazon.

The lesson? Affiliate marketing works best when your product needs education, trust and community endorsement.

How to Build an Affiliate Programme That Works (Without Getting Spammy)

Affiliate marketing can be a powerful tool – but only if it's done right. When brands take a hands-off approach, simply throwing up an 'affiliate sign-up' page and letting anyone join, they invite problems. Spammy bloggers looking for quick commission clicks, coupon sites that undercut brand value and low-quality traffic that doesn't convert into real customers can all flood the programme, doing more harm than good.

The best niche brands approach affiliate marketing with intention, carefully curating their partners and setting up systems that foster genuine advocacy.

1. Choose Affiliates Who Truly Align with Your Brand
Not everyone should be able to sign up. The most successful programmes partner with content creators, niche influencers and industry professionals whose audiences already trust them. These affiliates don't just push products – they share recommendations that feel organic and credible.

2. Make the System Seamless

An affiliate programme should be easy to use, both for the brand and its partners. Tracking commissions, managing referrals and keeping everything transparent builds trust and long-term engagement. Some of the best tools for affiliate marketing in India include:

- Rewardful (great for D2C and SaaS brands).
- Refersion (ideal for product-based businesses).
- GoAffPro (works well for Shopify-based brands).
- vCommission (India's largest affiliate network).

3. Go Beyond Just Cash Commissions

The best affiliate programmes offer more than just a percentage of sales. Top-performing affiliates are often rewarded with:

- Exclusive early access to new products.
- Higher commission tiers for consistent success.
- Personalized discount codes that they can share with their followers.

4. Don't Let Coupon Sites Take Over

Many large affiliate networks are overrun with discount-driven websites, which can weaken a niche brand's positioning. If your product isn't meant to compete on price, avoid relying too heavily on these sites – they might bring sales, but they can also erode your brand's perceived value.

5. Build Long-Term Relationships

Affiliate marketing isn't just about transactions; it's about trust. The best affiliates aren't one-time promoters – they're long-term ambassadors. Brands that invest in nurturing these relationships create a network of organic evangelists who genuinely believe in what they're selling.

A well-run affiliate programme doesn't feel like advertising – it feels like word-of-mouth at scale. And for niche brands, that's the most valuable kind of marketing there is.

The Power of Belonging: How Communities Make Niche Brands Unstoppable

A decade ago, if you were an avid sneakerhead in India, your options were limited. You could buy a pair of Nike Air Jordans from a store, but that was about it – there was no way to discuss sneaker drops, track rare releases or connect with others who shared the same obsession. Then something changed. Small, dedicated communities started forming – on Facebook, WhatsApp and, eventually, Discord. These were not mass-market groups where people casually talked about shoes. These were tight-knit, invitation-only spaces where hardcore collectors, resellers and sneaker enthusiasts swapped stories, debated colourways and made deals.

One of these communities, Mainstreet Marketplace,

started as a tiny WhatsApp group and eventually turned into India's first high-end sneaker resale store. But the real business wasn't just in selling sneakers – it was in creating a movement. Mainstreet didn't need a billboard or an expensive influencer campaign. It grew because its community was built around a simple but powerful idea: if you wanted to be part of India's sneaker culture, this was where you belonged.

This is the secret of niche businesses that build powerful, lasting brands. They don't just sell products. They create spaces where people feel seen, understood and connected.

Why Community Is the New Marketing Avenue

For years, businesses relied on advertising to reach customers. A brand would craft a message, push it out through television, print or social media and hope people would listen. But today, the most valuable marketing doesn't happen in public spaces – it happens in private conversations.

Hip hop singer Lil Nas X gave a concert on the gaming platform Roblox, which got 36 million views and helped sell merchandise worth millions of dollars. A Reddit forum, r/wallstreetbets, was responsible for the GameStop stock climbing to stratospheric levels.

Big brands still chase viral moments on Instagram and Twitter, but the real energy, the real cultural movements, are happening in digital campfires – small, interactive, closed communities. Whether it's WhatsApp groups for local bakers, Discord servers for NFT traders or Reddit forums for personal finance, people are spending more time in focused, interest-based communities than they are passively scrolling through mass-market content.

For niche businesses, this is an opportunity. Instead of competing with massive corporations for attention in crowded public spaces, they can go deeper – embedding themselves in smaller, more engaged communities where conversations actually matter.

How Communities Make Niche Brands Unstoppable

The strongest niche brands don't just attract buyers – they attract believers. People who see themselves in the brand. People who want to participate, not just purchase.

In India, Newme is trying to set up a clothing brand focused on millennials and Gen Z, but so is everyone else. Even global brands like Shein and Urbanic are entering India to target this demographic that makes up over half of India's population. Newme hopes that its community of users will make the difference. They have over half a million highly active followers on their Instagram page. They set up pop-up stores in high footfall areas and shoot videos of customers and post those online. This has become a hit with their customers. Customers are happy to promote their products and spread the word. Global brands like Lego, Harley-Davidson and Glossier have all done the same – turning customers into insiders, advocates and collaborators.

A great niche community does three things:

- It makes people feel like insiders – special, in-the-know, part of something exclusive.
- It fosters conversation – not just between brand and customer, but between members themselves.
- It turns customers into brand-builders – people who spread the message, answer questions and bring in new members.

These are not passive followers. These are co-creators of the brand's story.

Where Niche Brands Build Their Communities

1. Private Groups: WhatsApp, Discord and Telegram

Public social media is crowded and noisy. The real brand love happens in private spaces.

When The Whole Truth started gaining traction, it didn't just rely on traditional marketing. It built a loyalist community on WhatsApp, where customers could directly talk to the brand, get early access to new flavours and engage in real conversations about fitness and food transparency.

This approach creates intimacy and trust – customers feel like they're talking to a real person, not a faceless company.

Internationally, brands like Glossier and Supreme have done the same – keeping their most passionate customers close through invite-only groups and exclusive conversations.

2. Niche Reddit and Forum Communities: Owning the Conversation

Reddit is where obsessions turn into movements. Razer makes laptops, tablets and mice that are targeted at gamers. The good and bad of these products are discussed by users on Reddit. And Razer is there to participate in these discussions. In fact, all major games make or lose their markets in forums like Reddit and Twitch. This is true for Minecraft, Fortnite, Valorant and others. This is what helped Balatro, a poker-themed rogue-like deck-building game, take off so quickly.

The lesson? If people are already talking about your niche, be there – but add value.

3. Invite-Only Experiences: The Power of Scarcity

Not all communities are built online. Some of the most powerful ones exist in real life, through events, pop-ups and invitation-only meetups.

When Bira 91 launched as a niche craft beer brand in India, it didn't try to compete with Kingfisher on volume or price. Instead, it built a cult following through exclusive events, members-only tastings and insider perks for early adopters.

Luxury brands have used this playbook for decades

– think Rolex clubs, Soho House memberships or Tesla referral programmes. The best communities aren't open to everyone. They feel special, earned and worth being part of.

How to Build a Community-Driven Niche Brand

The best niche brands don't 'build communities'. They enable them – creating the spaces, tools and conversations that allow people to connect.

- Start with real engagement. Community doesn't happen overnight. It starts with real conversations – on WhatsApp, in forums, in events – before it scales.
- Encourage co-creation. Give customers a stake in the brand – whether it's voting on new designs (like Nike By You) or shaping product evolution (like The Whole Truth's flavour tests).
- Make membership feel valuable. The best communities feel earned – give insiders early access, exclusive perks or even just a title that makes them feel like part of something bigger.

The magic of community is belonging. A niche brand that creates a strong enough community doesn't need to chase customers anymore – the customers bring in new customers, and the brand becomes an identity, not just a business.

The most powerful brands aren't the ones with the loudest voices. They're the ones that make people feel like they belong.

- D2C channels empower niche brands by bypassing traditional retail gatekeepers and owning customer relationships.
- Websites are the digital flagship. They allow full control over branding, storytelling, pricing and data, unlike marketplaces that commodify products.
- Social media is a discovery engine. Niche brands use Instagram, Twitter, YouTube and LinkedIn not to broadcast, but to engage, educate and build community.
- The right influencers matter more than big influencers. Subject matter experts (SMEs), niche celebrities and micro-influencers build authentic trust and drive real sales.
- Affiliate marketing works for niche brands when it feels like word-of-mouth, not just sales-driven promotion.
- Communities drive long-term loyalty. Whether via WhatsApp, Discord, Reddit or real-world events, strong communities make customers co-creators.
- Be cautious with social media dependencies. Algorithm changes, there may be IP risks and platform bans can jeopardize growth.
- Successful niche brands thrive not by shouting louder, but by owning their message, choosing the right channels and building authentic relationships.

WHAT NEXT

11

FROM FRINGE TO FRONT PAGE

HOW NICHE BRANDS GO MAINSTREAM

On a warm afternoon in Delhi, sometime in 2015, a group of entrepreneurs stood in the aisle of a Big Bazaar, watching people shop. They weren't looking for anything specific – just observing. What did people pick up instinctively? What did they hesitate over? What did they ignore completely?

One of them noticed something odd. In the beverage section, people would stop, glance at the usual soft drinks – Coke, Pepsi, Frooti – but then move on, not quite convinced. When they did buy something, it was out of habit, not enthusiasm. There was no excitement in their choice.

This wasn't an accident. Something had changed. People were growing more conscious of what they consumed. They were starting to distrust artificial ingredients and preservatives. They wanted something different – but there was no real alternative on the shelves.

That's when Paper Boat found its moment. It didn't compete with Coca-Cola or Tropicana. It sidestepped the entire soft drink industry and created something entirely new – packaged, traditional Indian beverages that were healthy, free from artificial ingredients and rooted in childhood memories. Aam panna, jaljeera, kokum sharbat – flavours that had never been bottled before, but that every Indian remembered from childhood.

At first, Paper Boat was a small, niche brand, mostly found in airports, fancy cafés and gourmet stores. But as consumers became more conscious about what they consumed, the brand expanded its footprint. Today, it is a nationally recognized name, available in supermarkets and kirana stores across India.

This pattern is not unique. Many of India's most recognizable brands today started as niche businesses, catering to a small but passionate segment of consumers before expanding into the mainstream. What begins as a product for a select few often transforms into something that the mass market can't ignore – but only if the timing, strategy and cultural shift align.

Niche businesses don't stay small forever. The best ones find ways to scale – but they don't all follow the same path.

- Some grow because the niche itself explodes into the mainstream. What was once a niche interest suddenly becomes the default, pulling the business along with it.
- Others expand by branching into multiple niches, mastering one specialized market before moving to the next. They don't abandon their expertise; they replicate their success in parallel industries.
- Then some start niche but eventually go mainstream. They use their credibility in a specialized market as a launchpad, proving their value to a small, dedicated audience before making the leap to mass-market appeal.
- And some businesses never leave their niche at all. Instead, they scale by going deeper: expanding their product lines, refining their expertise and becoming so dominant that they turn their niche into an empire.

Niche Today, Ubiquitous Tomorrow

There's a pattern to how this happens. A brand begins with a specific, well-defined audience – one that cares deeply about something the mainstream market ignores. Over time, as consumer behaviour shifts and awareness grows, what was once niche becomes the new normal.

This was the case for Yoga Bar. When it launched in 2014, the idea of protein bars in India was practically non-existent. The few that did exist were expensive imports, mostly bought by gym-goers and serious fitness enthusiasts. The average Indian consumer never considered protein bars as a snack option. But something was changing. The health-conscious movement was growing, people were joining gyms and diets were shifting.

Yoga Bar positioned itself perfectly within this change – not just as a product, but as part of a larger movement around clean eating and better snacking. At first, it was purely D2C, targeting a niche fitness audience online. But as demand grew, it expanded into supermarkets and gyms. What started as a niche brand became a category leader, recently acquired by ITC.

A similar story played out in an entirely different industry with boAt, the brand that changed how India thinks about audio accessories. The headphone market was dominated by premium international brands like JBL, Sony and Bose. Indian consumers had two choices: pay a high price for a foreign brand or settle for cheap, unreliable knock-offs.

boAt saw the gap and filled it. They introduced stylish, premium-looking, affordable headphones specifically designed for Indian consumers – sweat-proof earphones for gym-goers, extra bass for Bollywood and EDM fans and stylish designs for young urban buyers. It started as a niche brand for music lovers who wanted good sound without spending a fortune. But as more people discovered the brand, it scaled rapidly, becoming India's largest audio accessories brand, even overtaking legacy players.

The lesson is simple: what begins as a niche product often ends up creating an entirely new category.

Why Some Niches Are Destined to Go Mainstream

Not every niche product becomes a mass-market success. The ones that do follow a pattern – they align with larger cultural or behavioural shifts that push them into the mainstream.

One of the biggest shifts in recent years has been the rise of health-conscious consumers, driving the success of brands like The Whole Truth, Sleepy Owl and Kapiva.

A decade ago, Indians weren't checking ingredient labels. Today, they're actively looking for chemical-free, organic and clean-label products. The Whole Truth capitalized on this by building trust through radical transparency – putting the exact ingredients on the front of the pack, instead of hiding them in fine print. It wasn't just a product – it was a statement against misleading food labels.

The same shift worked for Sleepy Owl, which introduced cold brew coffee to an audience that didn't even know it needed it. Cold brew coffee made specialty coffee smoother, less acidic and ready-to-drink anytime. Third-wave coffee culture was already on the rise in the West, and India's urban consumers were becoming more experimental. Sleepy Owl didn't just sell coffee; it sold a new way to experience coffee at home.

Another major shift has been the repackaging of Ayurveda for modern consumers. For decades, Ayurveda was associated with old-school medicinal brands like Dabur and Patanjali. Kapiva saw an opportunity to modernize Ayurveda, turning it into a lifestyle choice rather than a medical necessity. By focusing on functional wellness – gut health, weight loss and immunity – Kapiva made Ayurveda accessible to a younger, urban audience.

Similarly, WOW Skin Science took advantage of the clean beauty movement, offering toxin-free skincare without the traditional Ayurvedic aesthetic. Unlike Patanjali, which leaned into Ayurveda's past, WOW made it cool, modern and aspirational.

The success of these brands wasn't just about product innovation – it was about timing, storytelling and cultural momentum.

What Makes a Niche Brand Ready for the Big League?

- **A Growing Market Trend**: The niche has to align with where the world is going. Yoga Bar succeeded because fitness and protein awareness were rising. Kapiva grew because Ayurveda was shifting from medicinal to lifestyle wellness.
- **A Strong Brand Identity**: Niche brands win because they have a clear story. The Whole Truth wasn't

just about protein bars and protein powders – it was about radical honesty in food labelling.

- **D2C First**: Almost every brand that made it big started by selling online, building a dedicated base of loyalists before moving to retail.
- **A Product That Solves a Genuine Pain Point**: The best niche products feel obvious in hindsight. Of course, people wanted a clean-label protein bar. Of course, they wanted ready-made wedding wear. But someone had to be first to package and brand it right.

Every mainstream category we know today started as a niche. Plant-based diets were once fringe. Now they're everywhere. Even online education was once a niche. Now it's a billion-dollar industry.

For entrepreneurs, the lesson is simple: look at what small, passionate groups of people care about today. What's niche today will be mainstream tomorrow – and the brands that see it first will own the future.

Beyond the First Niche: How Businesses Expand from One Niche to Many

In the early 2010s, if you had heard of WOW Skin Science, it was likely for its sulphate-free shampoos. At a time when most Indian consumers were using chemical-laden hair products, WOW carved out a niche by offering natural, paraben-free alternatives. It wasn't as big as Dove or Pantene, but for those looking for clean beauty, it was a game-changer.

Fast forward to today, and WOW Skin Science has expanded far beyond hair care, entering multiple niches. It is now a major player in skincare, offering face washes, serums and sunscreens infused with natural ingredients. It has built a strong presence in body care, selling body butters, scrubs and shower gels that cater to those seeking luxurious, clean formulations. The brand has also tapped into health and wellness, with products like apple cider vinegar supplements and plant-based nutrition solutions. Even in men's grooming, WOW has carved out a space with beard oils, shampoos and face cleansers designed specifically for male consumers.

What started as a niche hair care brand has transformed into a multi-niche powerhouse, spanning beauty, wellness and personal care – proving that the demand for natural, chemical-free products isn't just a trend, but the future of consumer choices.

This is the story of multi-niche expansion – when a business that starts with a tight, specific audience finds a way to replicate its success across multiple customer segments without losing its identity. It's the natural next step for brands that master a niche and want to scale without becoming generic.

But it's also a tricky balancing act. Some brands do it brilliantly – expanding into adjacent markets while keeping their core DNA intact. Others overextend, diluting what made them special in the first place.

So, what separates the winners from the ones who lose their way?

Master One Niche Before Expanding

If there's one rule that holds across industries, it's this: you can't go multi-niche before you dominate a single niche first. Every brand that successfully expands into new niches first earns the trust and loyalty of a dedicated base before branching out.

Take HealthKart, for example. It started with a single product category – nutrition supplements. And not just any supplements – authentic, high-quality protein powders, vitamins and wellness products tailored for Indian consumers. It wasn't trying to compete with GNC or Amway in the traditional retail space. Instead, it sold directly to customers through its website, ensuring product authenticity, cutting out unnecessary markups and using data-driven marketing to target fitness enthusiasts and health-conscious buyers.

For the first few years, HealthKart didn't try to be everything to everyone. It focused entirely on building trust in the nutrition space, becoming the go-to platform for gym-goers and athletes looking for reliable supplements. Only after earning a loyal customer base did it expand into sports nutrition, weight management and general wellness. Today, it's not just a supplement retailer – it has successfully entered multiple related niches. In the three years from 2021 to 2024, its turnover jumped from ₹300 crore to over ₹1,000 crore.

The key here? The expansion felt natural. HealthKart didn't randomly jump from protein powders to cosmetics or home essentials. It grew strategically – moving into Ayurvedic health products, personalized nutrition solutions and even fitness accessories, all areas where its credibility made sense. By staying within the broader wellness ecosystem, HealthKart transformed from a niche supplement platform into a multi-niche fitness brand.

Find an Adjacency That Makes Sense

Not all niche expansions are successful. The ones that work have a clear logic to them – a common thread that ties the original niche to the new one.

WOW Skin Science started with hair care – a very specific niche catering to consumers looking for sulphate- and paraben-free shampoos that were gentle yet effective. For the first few years, its entire brand was built around natural ingredients, toxin-free formulations and transparency about what went into its products. Later, it expanded into skincare, body care and wellness. The key was that the core brand promise never changed – it was still about safe and natural products.

Contrast that with Byju's, which started as an EdTech company focused on test prep. It dominated that niche. But when it aggressively expanded into K-12 education, international markets, coding classes and upskilling courses, it started losing its core focus. The more it expanded, the more its brand felt bloated and stretched too thin.

A good multi-niche expansion should feel like an organic next step, not a desperate land grab.

Use Existing Customers to Validate the Next Niche

One of the best advantages of starting in a niche is that your first set of customers already trusts you. If you can successfully sell them a new product, you don't need to start from scratch in a new market.

This is exactly what Blue Tokai did. It built India's most recognizable specialty coffee brand, catering to urban, quality-conscious coffee drinkers. Instead of stopping at selling coffee beans and grounds, it expanded into cold brews, ready-to-drink cans and even café chains – all targeting the same coffee-loving customer base.

Similarly, Zymrat, a premium performance-wear brand, started with just moisture-wicking T-shirts and running shorts for athletes. Once it had built credibility among serious runners and fitness enthusiasts, it introduced training shoes, gym accessories and performance socks – all products its customers already needed.

The best multi-niche brands grow outward from a core, instead of trying to reinvent themselves with every new product.

When Multi-Niche Expansion Fails

For every brand that successfully expands into multiple niches, there's one that grows too fast and loses its way.

A cautionary tale is Snapdeal, which started as a niche daily deals platform but tried to take on Flipkart and Amazon head-on. Instead of sticking to its strengths, it expanded too broadly and lost its core identity, eventually fading into irrelevance.

The lesson? Expanding into multiple niches only works if you still have a clear brand identity. The moment a brand starts trying to be everything for everyone, it loses what made it special in the first place.

From Niche to Mainstream: How Small Brands Win Big

In 2016, if you had asked the average Indian consumer about boAt, they would have told you it was a cool, budget-friendly earphone brand. It wasn't Sony or JBL, but it looked premium, sounded great and didn't burn a hole in your pocket. It was the kind of brand college students and young professionals swore by.

Fast forward to today, and boAt is no longer just about earphones. It's a wearable tech company, a fitness brand, a fashion statement and an audio powerhouse rolled into one. It sells smartwatches, gaming headphones, wireless speakers and even grooming products. The brand that started by catering to young urban music lovers is now selling to gamers, runners and corporate executives alike.

In 2003, a small electric car start-up in California was struggling to stay afloat. Tesla wasn't a household name yet. In fact, most people dismissed the idea of electric cars as a fantasy for environmentalists – too expensive, too impractical and certainly not something the average driver would ever consider.

But Tesla didn't try to sell to everyone. Instead, it started with a niche product: a high-performance, all-electric sports car – the Tesla Roadster – aimed at wealthy, tech-savvy early adopters. The car was expensive and impractical for the mass market, but that didn't matter. It wasn't designed for mass appeal – it was designed to prove a point: that an electric car could be desirable.

The plan worked. The Roadster created hype, credibility and demand, giving Tesla the foundation to build the Model S, then the Model 3 and, finally, a full line-up of mainstream vehicles. Today, Tesla is one of the bestselling car brands in the world. But it didn't start by competing with Toyota or Honda. It started by owning a tiny, specific niche and then leveraging that success to move into the mainstream.

This is the power of starting specialized and scaling into mass-market dominance. It's a pattern that repeats across industries. Some brands understand the strategy and execute it flawlessly. Others try to jump too fast and lose their way.

Let's look at what separates the winners from those who stumble.

There's a reason why niche brands don't start mainstream. The mass market is brutal – filled with competitors, pricing pressure and deep-pocketed giants that can outspend any newcomer. Only when the niche is secured can the brand think of leveraging its credibility to expand into the broader mainstream market.

The companies that execute this strategy effectively follow a predictable pattern. They focus on a core group of early adopters who will not only buy the product but also advocate for it. This base of loyal customers provides the momentum needed for wider market acceptance.

From there, the brand uses its niche success to build credibility and awareness. With an established reputation, it can gradually expand – only when demand and brand strength are sufficient to support broader adoption. The key to successful expansion is ensuring that as the company moves into the mainstream, it does not lose sight of its original identity. The brand essence that made it appealing in the first place must remain intact, even as the audience grows.

Let's take the example of three companies that have done it well and one company that hasn't.

Amazon: From Books to Everything

When Jeff Bezos launched Amazon in 1994, he wasn't trying to build an empire. He was selling books. Books were the perfect niche product for an online store. They were standardized – a copy of *Pride and Prejudice* was the same everywhere, so customers didn't need to hold it in their hands before buying. They had an endless catalogue – something no physical bookstore could match. And, perhaps most importantly, book buyers were early adopters. They were tech-savvy, curious and willing to try something new.

For years, Amazon was just a bookstore. Bezos didn't rush to expand. Instead, he focused on perfecting the logistics of online retail – streamlining shipping, building recommendation algorithms and making customer service seamless. Only once Amazon had completely dominated the book market did it move into CDs and DVDs, then electronics, home goods and, eventually, everything. By the time Amazon became the 'everything store', it wasn't just another retailer – it was *the* online shopping destination. And it all started with books.

Veeba: The Condiments Powerhouse

Veeba's journey was different, but the pattern was the same. In its early days, Veeba wasn't on supermarket shelves, nor was it a household name. It was a behind-the-scenes player, supplying sauces and condiments to some of India's biggest fast-food chains – McDonald's, Domino's, KFC. Veeba built its reputation quietly, ensuring that its products were an integral part of the country's quick-service restaurant industry. It had scale, credibility and deep expertise long before consumers even heard its name.

When Veeba finally moved into mainstream retail, it didn't start with ketchup and mayonnaise. That would have been too obvious, too competitive. Instead, it launched premium salad dressings and international sauces – products that appealed to urban, health-conscious consumers. Only after establishing itself as a trusted name in premium condiments did it expand into more mainstream categories, competing directly with giants like Kissan and FunFoods. Today, Veeba is an FMCG powerhouse, but it didn't get there overnight. It moved step by step, ensuring that each expansion strengthened – not diluted – its credibility.

Wakefit: Mattresses and More

Wakefit's story followed a similar trajectory. It wasn't a furniture company when it started. It was a mattress brand. More specifically, it was a scientifically-backed, D2C mattress brand that offered orthopaedic memory foam mattresses at affordable prices. Unlike legacy players like Sleepwell and Kurlon, Wakefit didn't rely on traditional retail. It cut out the middlemen and spoke directly to young, urban consumers.

For the first few years, Wakefit stayed in its lane. It became *the* brand for high-quality, affordable sleep products. Only once it had won the trust of its customers did it expand – first into pillows, then bed frames, then sleep accessories. Eventually, Wakefit grew into a full-fledged home solutions brand, competing with Pepperfry and Urban Ladder. But it never made a sudden leap. It moved deliberately, ensuring that each new category felt like a natural extension of its expertise.

Byju's: Too Much Too Fast

Of course, not every company gets this right. The story of Byju's is a cautionary tale of what happens when a brand expands too quickly, without discipline. Byju's started as a premium test-prep platform, catering to serious students preparing for competitive exams. It was focused, high-quality and trusted. But then, instead of scaling methodically, it jumped into K-12 education, coding classes and even international markets – all at once.

With every expansion, Byju's diluted its brand. What had once been a premium, focused platform became known for aggressive sales tactics and a confusing product line-up. The company acquired multiple businesses in rapid succession, but instead of integrating them strategically, it became tangled in its expansion. Eventually, it ran into financial trouble. Byju's didn't fail because expansion was a bad idea. It failed because it abandoned its niche too soon and expanded without a clear, steady foundation.

The lesson is clear. The most successful brands don't try to be everything, everywhere, all at once. They start small. They find an opening that bigger players are ignoring. They dominate that niche, build trust and only then, when the time is right, do they expand. Amazon, Veeba, Wakefit and Tesla all followed this playbook. Byju's didn't. And that made all the difference.

Winning by Going Deeper: The Brands That Own Their Niche

There's a common belief in business that to grow, you need to expand – launch new products, enter new markets, chase a broader audience. But what if the best way to scale wasn't to grow outward, but to go deeper?

Some brands don't expand into new categories. They don't try to become mass-market giants. Instead, they double down on the niche they serve, becoming so dominant that no one else can seriously challenge them.

These brands don't just have customers; they have devotees. They are the name in their category, the brand that professionals trust, the default choice for anyone who takes their niche seriously.

This is the strategy of deep specialization – where instead of chasing scale, a company digs in, refining its products, strengthening its relationships and ensuring that its competitors can't even come close.

Let's look at three companies that have mastered this approach.

Stag: The Undisputed Champion of Table Tennis in India

In the world of Indian sports, table tennis has never been the main event. Cricket dominates, football has its pockets of loyalty and badminton has had its moments. But table tennis? It has always been a niche sport – played in school corridors, recreation centres and the occasional professional tournament. Most sports brands never saw the appeal. The market was too small, the audience too fragmented.

Stag saw it differently.

Rather than compete with global sportswear giants in running shoes or cricket gear, Stag made a singular bet: it would own table tennis in India. And not just one part of it – every part. Tables, bats, balls, nets, clothing, shoes – if it mattered to a table tennis player, Stag would make it.

The result? Walk into any sports facility in India, and you'll likely see a Stag table. At state and national-level tournaments, Stag equipment is everywhere. The brand has become more than just a supplier – it's a badge of identity for Indian table tennis players. From beginners picking up their first paddle to seasoned professionals training for international competitions, Stag is the name they trust.

It sells not just to individuals but to institutions – schools, universities, corporate offices and national sports academies. It doesn't need to branch into badminton or football to grow. Its strength comes from moving deeper into the world of table tennis, refining its products and ensuring that anyone who plays the sport in India plays it with Stag.

In an industry where most brands spread themselves thin, Stag stands out by going all in.

Steiner: The Optics of War

In the chaos of World War II, German engineer Karl Steiner had a vision – not to make binoculars for hobbyists or weekend adventurers but to build the most rugged, high-performance optics the world had ever seen. His goal was clear: to create binoculars that soldiers, sailors and security forces could rely on in the harshest conditions.

Steiner binoculars were never meant for casual birdwatchers. They were designed for military snipers, naval commanders and covert operatives – professionals who couldn't afford equipment failure. Every pair was built to withstand the extremes. They were shockproof and virtually indestructible, capable of surviving the brutality of the battlefield. They were engineered to be fog-proof and waterproof, functioning flawlessly in freezing rain, desert heat or open seas. And most critically, their lenses delivered crystal-clear visibility even in near darkness, allowing snipers and special forces to see when it mattered most.

Unlike other optics companies, Steiner never expanded into consumer electronics. It didn't start making cameras or telescopes. Instead, it doubled down on what it did best – engineering tactical and military-grade binoculars with relentless precision.

The result was dominance. Steiner became the supplier of choice for military forces around the world, trusted by those who operate in life-or-death situations. It established itself as the undisputed leader in the defence optics market, outpacing competitors who tried to serve both professionals and casual users. Today, if you need binoculars built for extreme conditions, Steiner is the only name that matters.

By refusing to chase mass-market appeal – by continuously perfecting its product for the most demanding users – Steiner has made itself irreplaceable.

Lindström: The King of Cleanroom Workwear

Most people don't think about industrial workwear. But in fields like pharmaceuticals, semiconductors and healthcare, the right clothing isn't just about comfort – it's about safety, compliance and precision. A single stray fibre in a microchip factory can ruin an entire production line. A poorly sanitized uniform in a hospital can spread infection. In these industries, contamination isn't an inconvenience; it's a disaster.

That's where Lindström comes in.

Lindström isn't just another uniform supplier. It specializes in cleanroom and technical workwear – garments designed for environments where even microscopic impurities pose a threat. Unlike mainstream apparel brands, it doesn't compete with Levi's or Adidas. It doesn't chase fashion trends or casual consumers. Instead, it owns one very specific niche: ultra-specialized industrial workwear.

Every piece of clothing Lindström provides meets the strictest hygiene and safety standards, ensuring workers in high-risk industries are protected. But it doesn't stop at just supplying garments. It offers full-service solutions, handling everything from delivery to decontamination, so companies never have to worry about whether their workwear is clean, compliant and ready for use. Over time, it has built deep partnerships with industries that rely on absolute cleanliness, embedding itself as a mission-critical supplier.

The result? Lindström isn't just a workwear company. It is the trusted partner for pharmaceutical firms, aerospace manufacturers and biotech companies – businesses where contamination can be catastrophic. By focusing on this highly specialized niche and perfecting every aspect of its service, Lindström has made itself indispensable.

The Strategy of Deep Specialization

These brands – Stag, Steiner and Lindström – prove that you don't have to go mass-market to scale. Instead, you can dominate by:

- Becoming the absolute best in one niche. Instead of doing many things well, do one thing flawlessly.
- Understanding your audience deeply. Talk to your core customers and be one among them, like Stag with TT players.
- Innovating within your category. Steiner doesn't sell binoculars on price – it sells them on unmatched performance in the toughest environments.
- Building a brand so strong that competitors don't stand a chance. Lindström isn't just a supplier – it is the default choice for cleanroom workwear.

Many brands fail because they try to do too much. They expand into new categories, dilute their expertise and end up competing in crowded markets where they no longer have an edge.

The smartest brands grow not by widening their reach, but by deepening their roots. When you dominate a niche so completely, you don't need to chase customers – customers come to you.

- **Niche brands grow in multiple ways**. Some ride cultural shifts (e.g., health-consciousness, clean beauty), others branch into related niches or scale by going deeper.
- **Brands like Paper Boat, boAt and Yoga Bar** succeeded by identifying emerging needs and building strong early loyalty.
- **Cultural tailwinds matter**. Kapiva, WOW and Sleepy Owl rode the wave of modern Ayurveda, clean eating and third-wave coffee respectively.
- **Going multi-niche works best after mastering one niche** – as seen with HealthKart, WOW Skin Science and Blue Tokai.
- **Expansion should feel logical**. New offerings must align with the brand's core values and customer base.
- **Cautionary tales like Byju's and Snapdeal** show the risk of expanding too fast without a solid foundation.
- **Deep specialization can also lead to dominance**, as with Stag, Steiner and Lindström, who built empires within narrow markets.
- **Niches grow through timing, trust and focus** – not by becoming everything to everyone, but by becoming indispensable to a few, then expanding smartly.

12

THE NEXT WAVE

WHERE NICHES ARE HEADED NEXT

If you look closely at the history of business, you'll notice a pattern. The companies that thrive aren't just the ones with the best products or the lowest prices. They're the ones that sense the undercurrents of change before anyone else. They don't just react to shifts in the market – they position themselves ahead of the curve, ready to capitalize on what comes next.

Niche businesses in India are at a crossroads. For decades, they have been defined by their ability to serve small, specialized markets with laser-sharp focus. But as the business landscape evolves, so does the meaning of 'niche'. The same forces that once kept these businesses small are now giving them unprecedented opportunities to scale, adapt and compete on levels never imagined.

The future of niche businesses will not be about remaining small and contained.

- It will be about leveraging the right tools to sharpen their advantage. Emerging technologies are reshaping how businesses identify and serve their ideal customers, breaking down traditional barriers to growth.
- The global marketplace is more accessible than ever, allowing niche brands to find audiences far beyond their local origins.
- In a world where consumers are more sceptical than ever, businesses that stand for something real – businesses that can prove their authenticity – will be the ones that win lasting loyalty.
- Tastes will change even more rapidly than they are now, shortening product cycles and increasing the need for product evolution.

This is the new reality for niche businesses in India. The ones that recognize these shifts and embrace them won't just survive – they will set the standard for what a niche business can achieve in the modern age.

The Future of Niche Businesses: How AI, Technology and Data Analytics Will Reshape the Landscape

In 2010, a small tea brand in Kolkata had an interesting problem. It made exquisite hand-rolled Darjeeling tea – floral, fragrant and delicate. But outside a handful of connoisseurs, no one seemed to care. Supermarket shelves were crowded with mass-market tea brands, and consumers reached for them out of habit. The company had two options: fight for shelf space in an indifferent market or find a way to make people care. It chose the latter.

Instead of relying on traditional retail, the company used data to find the right customers. It analysed purchase patterns, identified tea drinkers who valued craft and authenticity and started targeting them with digital campaigns. It used AI-powered recommendation engines to personalize offerings. Within a few years, Makaibari Tea, which was once a respected niche brand struggling for relevance, became an international success story.

This is the future of niche businesses in India.

For decades, the challenge of niche businesses has been discovery – how do you find the right customers in a world dominated by mass-market players? Traditionally, brands had to rely on intuition, word of mouth and sheer luck. But AI, technology and data analytics are changing everything. These tools are no longer the exclusive domain of tech giants and Silicon Valley start-ups; they are now accessible to anyone who knows how to use them. And for niche businesses, they are nothing short of revolutionary.

AI: The Ultimate Matchmaker

The old way of doing business was simple: create a product and hope the right people find it. The new way is different. AI doesn't wait for customers to come – it goes out and finds them.

Take, for example, the rise of hyper-personalized marketing. AI systems can now analyse vast amounts of data – browsing history, purchasing behaviour, social media interactions – and predict exactly what a consumer might want before they even know it themselves. A gourmet spice brand in Kerala doesn't have to advertise to everyone; AI can help it pinpoint the specific individuals who are actively searching for organic turmeric or single-origin black pepper.

Chatbots and virtual assistants are making niche businesses more efficient. Small companies that once struggled with customer support can now use AI-driven chat systems that answer questions, recommend products and even close sales – 24/7, without the overhead of a human sales team. What used to be a bottleneck is now an advantage.

The Data-Driven Niche

Data has long been described as the new oil, but for niche businesses, it's more like a GPS – showing them exactly where to go. In the past, small businesses had to rely on gut instinct to decide what to stock, how to price their products or which customers to target. Now, they don't have to guess. They can measure.

A craft beer company in Bengaluru can use data analytics to see which flavours are trending in different regions. A luxury handloom sari brand can analyse customer demographics to tailor its collections. A D2C fitness supplement start-up can A/B test product formulations before launching them at scale.

Even pricing – something once thought to be more art than science – is now optimized using data. AI-driven dynamic pricing tools adjust prices in real-time based on demand, competition and customer behaviour. A niche business no longer has to race to the bottom; it can find the exact price that maximizes both revenue and customer satisfaction.

Technology Levels the Playing Field

There was a time when running a niche business meant being small in every way – small reach, small operations, small impact. But technology is making it possible for niche brands to punch above their weight.

E-commerce platforms, powered by AI-driven logistics, allow a home-grown perfume brand in Jaipur to ship internationally with the same efficiency as a global giant. Subscription models – fuelled by predictive analytics – turn one-time buyers into lifelong customers. Even small-scale artisans are using augmented reality to let customers 'try on' jewellery or visualize furniture in their homes before they buy.

The biggest shift? Automation. Manufacturing, once a capital-intensive endeavour, is becoming more accessible through AI-powered production lines that reduce waste and increase efficiency. Niche businesses that once relied on third-party factories are now setting up lean, tech-driven operations that give them greater control over quality and innovation.

The Future Is Smart, but the Niche Stays Special

The fear with technology is always the same: will it make everything uniform? Will AI strip away the uniqueness that makes niche businesses special?

The reality is the opposite. AI and data don't erase niche appeal – they enhance it. They make it easier for brands to tell their stories, connect with their ideal customers and deliver better products without losing their essence. Makaibari Tea didn't have to become a generic company to succeed; it just had to find the right people, at the right time, with the right message.

That's the promise of the future. A world where niche businesses are not constrained by geography, resources or visibility. A world where technology doesn't replace craft but amplifies it. And a world where being small is not a limitation – but an advantage.

The Globalization Effect

There was a time when Indian businesses had to think small. Not in terms of their ambition, but in reach. If you were a niche brand making artisanal cheese in Himachal Pradesh or hand-forged kitchen knives in Tamil Nadu, your world was limited. You sold to local markets, maybe to a few urban speciality stores, but that was it. Scaling beyond borders? That was the domain of multinational giants with deep pockets and decades of global experience.

Not anymore.

Today, technology, trade and shifting consumer behaviour have redrawn the boundaries of business. A niche that was once confined to a neighbourhood or a city can now be global from day one. What was once a cottage industry can now find customers in California, Copenhagen or Kyoto. Globalization, long thought to be the playground of big business, is now the most powerful tool for the small and specialized.

Consider the transformation of Indian handicrafts. For generations, artisans in Rajasthan, Odisha and Gujarat crafted exquisite textiles, pottery and jewellery – pieces rich in history but often trapped in local economies. Their businesses depended on middlemen, government fairs and the occasional bulk order from an exporter. Then, e-commerce changed everything.

Platforms like Etsy, Amazon Global and even

Instagram allowed artisans to sell directly to international buyers. A weaver in Varanasi doesn't just have to depend on foot traffic in a local bazaar – she can now ship a custom Banarasi sari to a collector in New York. The walls between niche and mainstream, between local and global, are crumbling faster than ever before.

The Indian Niche, the Global Consumer

The second force at play is the shifting demand from consumers worldwide. In an era of mass production, buyers are searching for authenticity, for products with a story. They don't just want a spice mix; they want heirloom turmeric sourced from a single-origin farm in Kerala. They don't just want a cup of chai; they want a perfectly blended Makaibari tea that follows a 200-year-old family recipe.

Take the case of Ayurvedic beauty brands. A decade ago, Ayurveda was an 'Indian thing', respected but largely confined to domestic markets. Today, brands like Forest Essentials and Kama Ayurveda have cracked the global luxury market, positioning ancient wellness traditions as aspirational, premium and, most importantly, universal. The demand for Indian niche products is no longer limited to the diaspora; it comes from wellness enthusiasts in Berlin, sustainable fashion lovers in Los Angeles and skincare aficionados in Tokyo.

The Infrastructure of Globalization

But none of this would be possible without the invisible infrastructure supporting it. Logistics, payments and digital marketing have quietly become the backbone of the global niche economy.

Take shipping. Ten years ago, the idea of an independent coffee grower in Coorg selling directly to a café in Melbourne would have been a logistical nightmare. Today, with global fulfilment networks, integrated shipping application programming interfaces (APIs) and cross-border warehousing, that same grower can reach customers in days, not months. Payment systems like Razorpay and Stripe have eliminated friction, making it just as easy for an Indian business to accept payments from San Francisco as from Surat.

And then there's digital marketing. Social media has allowed niche brands to bypass traditional gatekeepers. With the right story and the right strategy, a micro-brand can gain cult status halfway across the world. Indian home-grown sneaker brands, artisanal chocolate makers and eco-friendly apparel start-ups aren't just selling products – they're building movements, amplified by digital storytelling and influencer networks that transcend geography.

The Next Wave: Hyper-Personalized Global Niche

The final shift combines data and globalization. The next generation of niche businesses will be hyper-personalized, able to tailor products not just to global markets but to specific individual preferences. An indie tea brand in Assam won't just export its blends – it will use AI to curate custom tea subscriptions for customers in different parts of the world, factoring in climate, taste profiles and health preferences.

Globalization, for niche businesses, is no longer about simply selling abroad. It's about making the world's consumers feel like they are part of something exclusive, something crafted just for them.

For decades, globalization favoured the massive – the multinational, the conglomerate, the corporation with the deepest supply chains. But the rules have changed. The future belongs to the agile, the adaptable and the deeply specialized. Indian niche businesses are no longer just serving local markets; they are becoming global brands, built on authenticity, craftsmanship and the power of digital reach.

The small is now mighty. And the niche? The niche is limitless.

The Age of Authenticity and Transparency

There was a time when businesses could hide behind slick marketing and carefully controlled narratives. A brand could say one thing, do another and get away with it. But those days are over. The internet remembers. Customers talk. And in an age where information moves faster than any corporate PR machine, authenticity and transparency aren't just ideals – they are survival strategies.

For niche businesses in India, this shift presents both a challenge and an opportunity. The challenge? There's nowhere to hide. If a brand claims to use organic ingredients but cuts corners, someone will find out. If a company promises ethical sourcing but relies on exploitative labour, it won't stay secret for long. But the opportunity? The brands that embrace radical transparency – those that open their doors, show their processes and stand by their values – have an unprecedented chance to build deep, lasting trust with their customers.

Authenticity as a Differentiator

Niche businesses thrive on specialization. They serve passionate, informed customers who care about the details. A craft coffee brand isn't just selling beans – it's selling the story of where those beans came from, how they were roasted and why they taste better than the mass-market alternatives. A D2C skincare start-up isn't just competing on price – it's competing on the purity of ingredients, the absence of chemicals and the ethical sourcing of materials.

But here's the catch: saying it isn't enough. Customers want proof. The brands that win in the future will be those that go beyond marketing claims and actually invite customers behind the scenes. Think QR codes that trace a product's journey from farm to factory. Think live-streamed production processes. Think founders who actively engage with customers on social media, answering tough questions instead of dodging them.

This is already happening with brands like Jaipur-based Khadi Essentials, which leans into transparency by showcasing the sourcing of its Ayurvedic ingredients. Or Sleepy Owl Coffee, which openly discusses its supply chain, roasting process and quality control measures. These brands understand that in a world of choices, authenticity is what makes them irreplaceable.

The Transparency Revolution

Transparency isn't just about being honest – it's about being proactively open. The best brands in the niche space are taking this to a new level, making transparency a part of their business model rather than a defensive response to scrutiny.

From day one, Raw Pressery differentiated itself by offering completely natural, preservative-free juices. But it didn't stop there – it made its nutritional information, sourcing and production processes completely open to customers. The result? A cult-like following of health-conscious consumers who didn't just buy the product but became evangelists for the brand, leading to a disruption in the beverage market.

boAt built its credibility not just by making high-quality headphones and speakers but by engaging directly with customers on social media, listening to feedback and refining its products based on real user insights. It doesn't pretend to be something it's not – it leans into its identity as a young, Indian, home-grown challenger brand. That honesty has made it one of the biggest consumer electronics success stories in India.

The Business Case for Radical Honesty

There's a reason why transparency is becoming a business imperative: it builds loyalty. When customers trust a brand, they don't just buy from it – they advocate for it. They tell their friends. They defend it against critics. And in a world where customer acquisition costs are skyrocketing, that kind of organic brand-building is priceless.

Niche businesses have an inherent advantage here. Unlike giant corporations that have to balance multiple stakeholder interests, niche brands are often founder-led, mission-driven and closer to their customers. They don't have to manufacture authenticity – it's already built into their DNA. The smartest ones will lean into this, using transparency as a way to not just differentiate themselves but to build communities around their brands.

In the next decade, the Indian consumer will only become more discerning. Access to global products, rising disposable incomes and increasing digital literacy mean that customers will demand more from brands. 'Trust us' won't cut it anymore. They'll want proof. They'll want to know not just what they're buying but who they're buying from and what those companies stand for.

For niche businesses, the future belongs to those who embrace this shift. Those who open their books, share their values and prove – day after day – that they are exactly who they claim to be. Because in a world of endless choices, the brands that win won't necessarily be the biggest or the cheapest.

They'll be the ones that customers believe in.

The Acceleration of Taste: How Changing Preferences Will Shape India's Niche Businesses

In 2019, a start-up in Mumbai launched a line of artisanal kombucha. It was the kind of product that, a decade earlier, would have been met with blank stares. But within months, demand skyrocketed, driven by social media influencers and health-conscious urbanites. By 2023, the brand had expanded into probiotic sodas and kefir. Then, almost overnight, sales plummeted. What happened? Tastes changed.

This, as it turns out, is the defining challenge for niche businesses in the years ahead. If transparency and authenticity are becoming the foundation of trust, then adaptability is becoming the foundation of survival.

The Shrinking Lifespan of Trends

For most of the twentieth century, tastes evolved slowly. Fashion cycles lasted a decade, food preferences changed gradually and businesses had time to adapt. Today, that timeline has collapsed. What once took years now happens in months. A viral TikTok video can launch a new flavour, fabric or fitness trend overnight – and render it obsolete just as quickly.

Take the case of craft gin in India. For a few years, home-grown distilleries like Greater Than and Hapusa were the toast of the urban elite. Restaurants curated elaborate gin menus. Home mixologists experimented with botanicals. Then, suddenly, Mezcal became the next big thing. And soon after, low-alcohol and alcohol-free spirits started gaining traction. The speed at which preferences shift is increasing, and niche businesses can no longer afford to be static.

The Netflix Effect on Consumer Choice

One way to understand this acceleration is through the lens of entertainment. Think about how we consumed movies in the 1990s. A blockbuster could dominate theatres for months. Today, on streaming platforms like Netflix and Amazon Prime, a film might trend for a week before disappearing into obscurity. The same phenomenon is happening in food, fashion, beauty and even wellness. Consumers are bombarded with choice, and novelty is rewarded.

This presents a paradox for niche businesses. The very thing that makes them successful – being unique – can also make them vulnerable. If a brand builds its identity around a single product or aesthetic, it risks obsolescence the moment consumer preferences shift.

So, what does this mean for niche businesses in India? The ones that thrive in the future will not just be authentic; they will be agile. They will design their business models for rapid iteration, experimentation and reinvention.

Consider a Delhi-based slow fashion label that started with handwoven linen shirts. Five years ago, that would have been enough. Today, the brand needs to anticipate that customers may soon prefer plant-based leather, upcycled denim or biodegradable fabrics. The most successful niche brands will no longer just sell a product; they will sell a mindset – one that embraces change as a core value.

Strategies for Surviving the Fast-Changing Marketplace

1. **Modular Offerings**: Businesses will need to design products and services that can be easily tweaked. A health food start-up that sells millet-based snacks should be prepared to pivot to sorghum, fonio or a new super grain that gains popularity next year.

2. **Micro-Trends, Not Mega-Trends**: Instead of chasing mass-market adoption, future-focused brands will target smaller, fast-moving subcultures. A Chennai-based tea brand might launch limited-edition flavours every quarter, tapping into short-term curiosities rather than committing to a single bestseller.
3. **Real-Time Consumer Feedback**: The traditional model of conducting market research and launching a product a year later will be too slow. Brands will rely on live data – social media polls, direct customer interactions and AI-driven insights – to tweak offerings instantly.
4. **A Narrative of Evolution**: Consumers are more forgiving of change when they see it as intentional. Brands that openly document their evolution – through behind-the-scenes storytelling – will retain loyalty even as they shift their offerings.

The Inevitable Acceleration

If there is one certainty about the future, it is that change will come faster than ever before. Niche businesses that succeed in the coming years will not just be those that have a strong identity, but those that recognize identity itself as fluid. The brands that win will not just anticipate change; they will embody it.

In the marketplace of tomorrow, the only thing more valuable than uniqueness is the ability to reinvent it.

- **Niche businesses are entering a new era**, driven by AI, data and global access – where small no longer means limited.
- **AI and analytics** help brands precisely identify, target and personalize offerings for micro-audiences, increasing impact without mass-market budgets.
- **Technology levels the field**. Small brands can now match large firms in logistics, manufacturing and customer engagement through automation and smart tools.
- **Globalization is a growth engine**. Indian niche brands can now sell worldwide, as consumers crave authenticity, storytelling and culturally rich products.
- **Transparency builds trust**. Consumers demand openness on sourcing, processes and ethics. Brands that show, not just tell, win loyalty.
- **Tastes are evolving faster than ever**. Brands must be agile, experimenting with trends, formats and messages to stay relevant.
- **The future of niche business in India lies at the intersection of craft and code** – authenticity powered by intelligence, local roots with global ambition and constant reinvention.

ACKNOWLEDGEMENTS

Writing *The Niche Code* has been both a professional and deeply personal journey. I owe my first and most heartfelt thanks to my family, especially my parents, who instilled in me the values of resilience and curiosity that have carried me through both entrepreneurship and academia. Their unwavering support and belief in me have been the foundation of everything I do.

I thank my wife and my children for their patience and support, and especially for the critical feedback they gave so readily, even when it was not easy for me to hear. I thank my sister for the many conversations that sparked and shaped several of the central ideas in this book.

I thank my colleague Rachna Tiwari for helping me set up meetings with several of the founders and others whose stories appear in this book. I am also grateful to my colleague and friend Sam Placid for being the sounding board I so often needed and for reminding me that no idea is too small to be shaped into something meaningful.

I owe a debt of gratitude to Anjali Yadav and Rahul Sarkar for their help in my research and for patiently digging out material that has enriched the narrative. My friends at TiE Delhi and at CII – Young Indians have also played a crucial role, opening doors and making the connections that were so necessary to bring this book alive.

I am grateful to all my students and colleagues from over the years, whose questions, debates and insights sharpened my thinking and kept me grounded in the realities of business. Many of the stories and frameworks in this book were shaped in classrooms, incubators and late-night discussions with young entrepreneurs daring to dream. I also want to thank the entrepreneurs who shared their journeys with me with candour and courage – you have lent this book a heartbeat.

I am also deeply grateful to my agent Anish Chandy for believing in me and actually liking what I write. My heartfelt thanks to Pujitha Krishnan and the team at Pan Macmillan India for believing in this idea and helping me shape it into something solid and accessible.

REFERENCES

'10 Niche and Luxury Homegrown Brands to Look Out for in 2025', *Harper's Bazaar India*, 13 June 2025. Available at https://www.harpersbazaar.in/fashion/story/10-niche-and-luxury-homegrown-brands-to-look-out-for-in-2025-1223491-2025-06-13.

'India's Space Start-Ups Exploring Niche Markets, Global Collaborations', *Times of India*, 9 July 2023. Available at https://timesofindia.indiatimes.com/business/startups/companies/indias-space-start-ups-exploring-niche-markets-global-collaborations/articleshow/101612690.cms.

'One 97 Communications (Paytm Ltd) – Stock Quote & Financials', *Moneycontrol*, 22 July 2025. Available at https://www.moneycontrol.com/india/stockpricequote/online-services/one97communicationspaytm/OC03.

'Vedant Fashions – Stock Quote & Financials', *Moneycontrol*, 22 July 2025. Available at https://www.moneycontrol.com/india/stockpricequote/retailing/vedantfashions/VF04.

Aditi Bhatia-Kalluri, 'E-commerce for Rural Micro-Entrepreneurs: Mapping Restrictions, Ecologies of Use, and Trends for Development', *Development Studies Review,* vol. 32(5), 22 August 2021, 398–423. Available at https://arxiv.org/abs/2108.09759.

Aidin Salamzadeh, 'Start-up Boom in an Emerging Market', *Competitiveness in Emerging Markets: Market Dynamics in the Age of Disruption*, ed. D. Khajeheian, Mike Friedrichsen, Wilfried Mödinger (Cham: Springer Nature, 2018), 233–43.

Alexandra Sheehan, 'What Is a Niche Market? Top 11 Examples in 2025', *Shopify India Blog*, 12 March 2025. Available at https://www.shopify.com/in/blog/niche-markets.

Anjali Chopra, A. Pandey, R. Iyer and S. Puri, *Mamaearth: Navigating Growth Beyond Baby Care* (Canada: Ivey Publishing, 2023).

Anurag Prasad and Judhajit Basu, 'Brothers Ping Pong', *Fortune India*, 5 July 2011. Available at https://www.fortuneindia.com/people/brothers-ping-pong/101021.

Brittany Nguyen, 'WeWork's Rise To $47 Billion—And Fall To Bankruptcy: A Timeline', *Forbes*, 6 November 2023. Available at https://www.forbes.com/sites/brittanynguyen/2023/11/06/weworks-rise-to-47-billion-and-fall-to-bankruptcy-a-timeline/.

David Curry, 'Airbnb Revenue and Usage Statistics', *Business of Apps*, updated 24 February 2025. Available at https://www.businessofapps.com/data/airbnb-statistics/.

Dawn Thilmany, 'What are niche markets? What advantages do they offer?', *Assessment and Strategy Development for Agriculture,* vol. 8(13), 2012, 1–14. Available at https://

valueaddedag.org/nichemarkets/01whatarenichemarkets.pdf.

Emily Selter, '11 Things You Didn't Know About Birkins', *Town & Country Magazine*, 4 October 2023. Available at https://www.townandcountrymag.com/style/fashion-trends/g10262999/hermes-birkin-bag-facts/.

Ginesys, 'Explore India's Top Niche Marketplaces for E-commerce Growth in 2025', *Ginesys Retail Blog*, 15 June 2025. Available at https://www.ginesys.in/blog/new-niche-marketplaces-explore-india-2025.

H. R. Pulliam, 'On the Relationship Between Niche and Distribution', *Ecology Letters*, vol. 3(4), 2000, 349–61.

H. Vandermeer, 'Niche Theory', *Annual Review of Ecology and Systematics*, vol. 3, 1972, 107–132. Available at https://www.annualreviews.org/content/journals/10.1146/annurev.es.03.110172.000543.

Jonathan Selvaraj, 'Paris Olympics: The Undisputed Victor of Olympic Shooting – Nilesh Rane's Capapie', *The Hindu*, 20 July 2025. Available at https://www.thehindu.com/sport/olympics/paris-olympics-the-undisputed-victor-of-olympic-shooting-nilesh-ranes-capapie/article68451170.ece.

R. Raviprakash, M. Singh, A. Mehta, S. Kulkarni et al., 'Using Artificial Intelligence for Economic Upliftment of Indian Handicraft Industry', *International Journal of AI and Society*, vol. 34(4), 2019, 223–38. Available at https://arxiv.org/abs/1907.02014.

Rinchen Norbu Wangchuk, 'Ghazal Alagh's Mamaearth Unicorn Startup Inspired by Son', *Better India*, 20 May

2022. Available at https://thebetterindia.com/286022/ghazal-alagh-mamaearth-unicorn-startup-inspired-by-son-women-entrepreneurs/.

S. K. Das, 'Investigating Circularity in India's Textile Industry: Overcoming Challenges and Leveraging Digitization for Growth', *Journal of Sustainable Business*, vol. 11(1), 2025, 45–68. Available at https://arxiv.org/abs/2501.15636.

Shelley Singh, 'Niche Online Players Like Lenskart, Fabfurnish Catering to Specific Needs of Consumers', *Economic Times*, 16 August 2014. Available at https://economictimes.indiatimes.com/tech/internet/niche-online-players-like-lenskart-fabfurnish-catering-to-specific-needs-of-consumers/articleshow/40312451.cms.

Sudhir Chowdhary, 'Industry Start-ups: Niche Eyewear Tech Under Fine Lens', *Financial Express*, 23 August 2018. Available at https://www.financialexpress.com/business/industry-start-ups-niche-eyewear-tech-under-fine-lens-1227488/.

T. Dalgic and M. Leeuw, 'Niche marketing revisited: concept, applications and some European cases', *European Journal of Marketing*, vol. 28(4), 1 April 1994, 39–55. Available at https://doi.org/10.1108/03090569410061178.